LAUGHING OUT LOUD

LAUGHING OUT LOUD

MYRON COHEN

with drawings by SHEILA GREENWALD

THE CITADEL PRESS • NEW YORK

PN6162
.C64

First Printing, November, 1958
Second Printing, November, 1958
Third Printing, December, 1958
Fourth Printing, December, 1958
Fifth Printing, December, 1958
Sixth Printing, January, 1959
Seventh Printing, August 1960

Dedication

TO THE TIRED BUSINESSMAN . . . WHO'S ALWAYS
CHASING HIS SECRETARY AROUND THE OFFICE . . .
NOW YOU KNOW WHY HE'S TIRED!

PREFACE

Material has always played an important role in my life. A comedian needs good material if he's going to get laughs, just as a silk salesman needs good material if he's going to sell his product. And that's what I was before I became a comic—a silk salesman.

Without boasting, I'd like to say that I was probably the most popular silk salesman in the Garment Center—and the poorest one, too.

Every time I'd approach a prospective customer and try to sell him silk, he'd ask if I knew any new jokes. Of course, I did. Then I'd tell him one, he'd tell me one, I'd tell him another . . . and thus it went all day. Finally, he'd say, "Myron, you're great. You ought to be on the stage."

But when I'd ask him about buying some silk, he'd shrug his shoulders and say, "Sorry, Myron, but busines is bad and I. . . ." Then, instead of feeling blue, I'd say something like, "Speaking about business, did you hear the one about the salesman who was stranded in a small backwoods town due to a critical power shortage who wired his boss: I DON'T KNOW WHEN I'LL BE ABLE TO GET OUT OF HERE. IT MIGHT TAKE WEEKS. Upon receiving the

7

wire, the head man immediately replied, AS OF TODAY YOU START YOUR TWO WEEKS VACATION."

Meanwhile, whenever there was a smoker, a banquet, or any other affair, I was always invited to perform . . . for nothing, of course!

Finally, after much coaxing by my associates, I decided to try my luck professionally.

When all the great comedians heard that I was starting out, they came to my aid. First Danny Thomas sent me some jokes. Jimmy Durante sent me some jokes. George Jessel sent me some jokes. And Jack Benny . . . he sold me some jokes.

And that, dear reader, is how a silk salesman became a spinner of yarns.

CONTENTS

LAUGHING OUT LOUD

GARMENT GAIETIES

Whenever I hear anyone use the term, "The Garment Jungle," I always feel that the speaker has missed the boat and the point —it's always said sardonically out of the side of the mouth. This just isn't *my* Garment Center—a world gilded for me by wonderful memories and continuing pleasant associations. The Garment Center has been good to me. After all, I got my start telling stories at Garment Center socials—like many another comedian who apprenticed in the Catskills or small night clubs.

Yes, I grew up in the Garment Center, developed my style in the Garment Center, got my experience in the Garment Center, and although I don't get too many opportunities to frequent my old haunts, I'm proud to have once been associated with all the wonderful people in the clothing business.

As I said in my preface (if you're one of those people who don't skip over prefaces), I was trying to be a silk salesman when the show business bug bit me and caused the worm to turn. One day I just decided to give up pushing silk and become a *full-time* comedian.

I was working for A. E. Wullschleger at the time. Let me hasten to explain that Wullschleger had been a wonderful boss. After all, he laughed at my jokes even if he didn't pay me, so my decision had nothing to do with him.

But he *was* my boss, so it wasn't the easiest thing to do to go in and tell him I was quitting. I squared my padded shoulders, stuck out my chin and strode into his office. Henry Roth, his junior partner, was there.

I must have looked funny because Henry asked, "Anything wrong, Myron?"

"Well, yes and no," I faltered. "It's just that I'm—I'm leaving."

"Leaving?" Wullschleger looked up, surprised. "You got a better job?"

"You might call it that," I told him. "I'm becoming a full-time comedian."

Wullschleger didn't look impressed. "And how much are they paying you?"

That look and tone got me. "Oh, about $1250 a week," I said nonchalantly.

He was incredulous. "For that guff you tell? . . . that—that *trash* you say?"

I've been with you for more than two years now. Would $15 be all right?"

"Fifteen dollars!" shouted the manufacturer. "What do you think I am, a millionaire?"

☺

Then there is the one about the mother who was telling her friend about her three sons.

"Sammy is a doctor," she said.

"Is that right?"

"Ben is a lawyer."

"I'll bet you're proud of him, too."

"And Joe is a silk manufacturer."

"A silk manufacturer?"

"Yeah, and you know what? He supports Sammy and Ben."

☺

Bosses in the garment industry are always worrying about business. Of course, this is a common disease in every line of endeavor, but Garment Center businessmen seem to have the most acute cases.

Recently, Randy and Mel Rosenthal, of Rona Dress, told me about the two partners, Irving and Bob, who owned a small business in the Garment Center.

One afternoon, the pair, who oddly enough were good friends, went rowing in Central Park. It was a beautiful day and they floated to the middle of the lake. Suddenly, right in the middle of the water, the boat developed a leak and overturned. When the spray cleared, Irving was sitting on the upended boat and Bob was struggling in the water.

"Irving, help me!" Bob yelled, "I can't swim!"

His partner looked around. "Wait a minute, I'll get help," he said. "Can you float alone?"

Struggling valiantly to stay above water, Bob sputtered, "A time like this and you want to talk business?!"

☺

Irving and Max met walking down Seventh Avenue.

"How's business?" asked Max.

"Well, you know how it is," replied Irving, "business is like sex. When it's good, it's wonderful. When it's bad, it's still pretty good."

☺

Ginsberg and Levy met each other on the train to Philadelphia. They had been schoolboy companions and hadn't seen each other for nearly twenty years.

"How are you, Ginsberg?" asked Levy. "Where are you going?"

"Me, I'm going to Philadelphia."

"So am I."

"Is that so? And what business are you in?"

"I'm a silk salesman. And you?"

"What do you know about that! I'm a silk salesman, too."

"Ginsberg, do you remember the great times we used to have at those parties at Rose Lieberman's house in Brooklyn and how we used to fight over Rose? Remember those parties, old man?"

"I'll never forget them."

They continued reminiscing, but half of Ginsberg's mind was busy elsewhere. Somehow everything didn't seem kosher to him. He began to think:

"This Levy is a smart guy. He says he's going to Philadelphia, but why should he tell me the truth? He's in the same business. I'll bet he's going to Pittsburgh. Why should he go to Pittsburgh? He must be going to see Abe Cohen. Abe is probably going to place a big order for silk and he's trying to get the whole thing.

18

"No, that can't be. He must know that Abe Cohen always divides his order among three of his favorite salesmen. Maybe he's going to see Max Gold. No, Max placed his order weeks ago. Say, wait a minute, Lieberman and Sons moved from Brooklyn to Pittsburgh, and old Lieberman is Rose's father. What did he bring up Rose for? I bet he still has a case on her. That's it. He's going to Pittsburgh to get himself engaged to Rose Lieberman."

He turned to his friend. "Congratulations you old faker, you!" Ginsberg chuckled.

"How did you know?" gasped Levy.

Ginsberg shrugged, "It stands to reason!"

Sam Frontman, of Paramount Dresses in Philadelphia, knew a Garment Center cutter who approached his boss and asked, "Could I have Thursday off? It's my silver wedding anniversary."

The boss snarled, "Do I have to put up with this every twenty-five years?"

George and Wally, my haberdashers, had a friend who opened a men's clothing store in the Garment Center. About a week after he opened, the fellow was shocked when a hysterical woman raced into his store.

"This shirt I bought for my husband has a hole in it."

"Well, what do you expect me to do?"

"I'd like to get my money back."

"There are no refunds here, lady."

"No refunds! What about this notice right on the sales slip: MONEY CHEERFULLY REFUNDED IF NOT SATISFACTORY?"

"Sure," said the fellow, "but there was nothing wrong with your money."

☺

A big business tycoon died and went to his eternal resting place.

When he arrived in the other world, he was greeted by a salesman who used to visit him on earth.

The salesman greeted him with a big hello. "Max, ole boy, I'm here for the appointment."

"What appointment?" barked the businessman.

"Don't you remember?" asked the salesman. "Every time I used to try to see you at your office, you'd tell me you'd see me here."

☺

A Garment Center manufacturer was interviewing applicants to replace his private secretary who was resigning because of expectant motherhood. His right-hand man sat with him as he looked the applicants over.

The first girl was a beautiful buxom blonde. She turned out to be intelligent and had excellent secretarial skills. The second was a dark-haired beauty who was even more intelligent and proficient than the first. The third one was cross-eyed, had buck teeth, and weighed 190 pounds.

After interviewing all three candidates, the boss informed his associate that he was hiring the third applicant.

"But why!" asked the astonished employee.

"Well," boomed the boss, "in the first place, she looked very intelligent to me. In the second place, it is none of your damned business. And in the third place, she's my wife's sister."

☺

Calvin, of the T.V. Coffee Shop, swears this happened: After discovering that he had had a very poor season, the angry manufacturer walked into his office and shouted, "Why is it that every time I walk into this office, I find that nobody is working!"

"Simple," came a voice from the back, "it's those damned rubber heels you wear."

☺

Two Garment Center partners once hired a new secretary. The girl was extremely pretty but very dumb.

"One day," said the first partner, "I asked her to get me the phone number of Zelda Zinc."

"And you know what?" added the other, "Two hours later I came out and asked her how she was doing with that phone number."

"I'm doing fine," she said, "I'm up to the D's already!"

☺

The boss of a big dress house took his wife to Florida for a vacation. He decided that he would like to go by car and see the various states along the way.

During the first day out, they ran into a brutal storm and had to pull into the nearest motor court. As they did so, a young attendant came out and was about to give them a room when an old woman peeked out of a door.

"Do they have a marriage license, Fred?"

"No, we don't."

"When were you married?" the woman demanded.

"Uh, in September, 1938," the husband replied.

"Idiot!" the wife snapped. "It was October 14, 1939!"

"Let them have the room," said the old lady. "They're married."

☺

As Jack Silverman, of the old Roumanian put it: a shoulder strap is "a little piece of ribbon designed to keep an attraction from becoming a sensation."

☺

And then there's the Harry Hershfield classic about the big manufacturer who walked into a clothing store and told the salesman, "I like that suit in the window. What are you asking for it?"

"This is a high class establishment," the salesman told him, "I'm not going to say $100, $90, $85 . . . with me, it's one price —$80."

"Isn't that funny," said the manufacturer, "I'm exactly the same nature. I'm not going to say $75, $70, then $65. By me it's one price also—$50."

"Sold."

☺

Nat Sherman, who supplies the Garment Center with all those cigars and cigarettes, knows a salesman who has 100 suits . . . and they're all pending.

☺

After a particularly dismal season, an associate of furrier George Becker was trying to cheer up his partners. "After all, fellows," he said, "we have to be optimistic. The only thing we have to fear is fur itself."

☺

Marcia Parker and Bill Felstein, of the Junior House of Milwaukee, attended a party where they met an old acquaintance.

"Hello Sam," greeted Bill, "how's business? I heard that you lost a lot on that fall shipment of dresses. Is that true?"

"It's true."

"And that you almost went bankrupt?"

"That's true, too."

"But I understand you made a big profit on another shipment and wound up having had a pretty good season."

"That's right. Then you heard about it, Bill."

"Yeah," said Bill, "but this is the first time I'm hearing all the details."

☺

Abe Goodman once employed a cutter who was always having hard luck. The fellow invariably seemed to be in debt, and as time went on his bills grew larger and larger. Finally, he reached a point at which he had to do something drastic. Winter was coming, and he couldn't afford to buy overcoats for his three young children.

In desperation, the fellow broke into another firm's storeroom and stole three coats. While he was making his escape, he was caught.

Brought before a judge, he told his story. "I'm not a criminal, your honor. I only stole to keep my children from freezing to death. Is that a crime?"

Then the manufacturer who owned the dress house which was burglarized was called to the stand.

"Do you wish to press charges against this man?" asked the man on the bench. "Or would you rather settle this matter out of court?"

"I want to press charges," the manufacturer said sternly.

The judge was surprised. "But he's not really a criminal."

"Listen, Judge," began the fellow. "If he would have taken those coats last week, I wouldn't have cared, and if he'd taken them next week, I wouldn't have cared. But this week, I'm taking inventory!"

Boris and Joe Alper of Glass and Company love the one about the rich manufacturer who married his secretary and went to Florida on their honeymoon.

No sooner had they checked into their hotel room than a rough-looking thug climbed through the window and poked a gun in the manufacturer's ribs.

"This is a stickup," the fellow announced.

Then he drew a circle on the rug with his heel and gruffly ordered the groom to stand inside it.

"Move one inch outside," snarled the crook, "and I'll pump lead into you."

Then the fellow stuffed his pockets with their jewelry, money, and other valuables. Next, he embraced the sobbing bride and made violent love to her.

"How could you just stand there," wailed the girl later, "and watch a monster like that make love to me? What are you, a man or a mouse?"

"I'm a man, of course. And I didn't just stand there, either. Every time he had his back turned, I stuck my foot outside the circle."

☺

Morris Degan, president of the Gilatzyaner Association, had a friend who approached his lawyer and told him, "I won't pay you unless you are certain that there are grounds for legal action."

"Well, tell me the case," asked the lawyer.

The fellow explained the whole situation and when he had finished, he asked the mouthpiece what he thought.

"The case is airtight," the lawyer informed him. "The other fellow hasn't a leg to stand on. My advice will cost you $100, and for an additional $150, I'll start suit."

"No," said the fellow, "I guess I'd better not."

"But why?" demanded the lawyer.

"Because I gave you the other fellow's side of the story!"

☺

In the Garment Industry, as in all other industries, the workers feel that they're not appreciated by the boss. Charlie Morris often tells the one about the faithful cutter, who after 25 years of work, approached his boss and asked him for a raise.

"Well," began the head man, "business is bad now, Sam, and I just can't afford to give you a raise."

"But I'm doing three men's work, and I always have," retorted the sad Sam.

"Three men's work!" exploded the boss. "Tell me who the other two men are, and I'll fire them!"

☺

Henry Blank of Lehigh Frocks tells about the Garment Center cutter who stormed into his boss's office and screamed, "I've been killing myself for you! I want a raise!"

His boss looked up calmly, smiled, and said, "Why Ben, there must be some mistake. I gave you a raise three weeks ago."

"You did?" exclaimed the embarrassed Ben. "And my wife never even told me!"

☺

Models, as I stated before, are a very important part of the Garment Center. Thousands of words, both fact and fiction, have been written about these shapely lasses.

Agent Phil Consolo overheard a model being interviewed by

her prospective boss. "What are you around the neck, Miss Green?"

"Twelve," she replied.

"What are you around the hips?"

"Thirty-three," she smiled.

"And how are you around the waist?"

"Just wonderful," she cooed.

☺

Al Rosenstein of Roseweb Frocks had a model who once told him: "The nicest thing about money is that it never clashes with anything you're wearing."

☺

A garment manufacturer, who was quite a wolf, grew extremely fond of one of his new models, a remarkably comely lass.

One day when she was coming out of the fitting room, he approached her, gave her a peck on the neck and whispered, "How about coming up to my beach house for the weekend? We'll have loads of fun."

"All right," she smiled. "And I'll bring my boy-friend."

"Your boy-friend? What for?"

"In case your wife wants to have some fun, too!"

☺

Two prosperous Garment Center manufacturers hired a new model. She was beautiful but she wasn't too bright. The two partners were attracted to the girl, but the interest was not of the paternal nature.

"Look," one told his partner, "being that she's so young and pretty, she might be taken advantage of by some fast-talking fellow. I think we ought to take it upon ourselves to teach her what's right and what's wrong."

"You're right," agreed his partner. "You teach her what's right."

☻

Al Frischer of Frischer Carpet Co. employed a young salesman who took a pretty model to see "A Streetcar Named Desire" at one of those off-Broadway theatres. As soon as they found their seats, the girl excused herself and looked for the powder room. Since the theatre was in an old building, the poor girl wandered through winding corridors for several minutes until she finally found the place. It was empty except for a girl seated on a sofa. The model quickly fixed her make-up, adjusted the seams of her stockings, took a final glance in the mirror and with the remark, "God, I look a mess tonight," departed.

Then she went back into the corridor and found her way back to her seat. As soon as she arrived, she asked her boyfriend, "What happened?"

"Not much," he told her, "one girl was sitting on a sofa, then some girl walked in, fixed her stockings and said, 'God, I look a mess tonight,' and walked off."

☻

Noel Kramer, manager of Rock 'n Roll singers, knew the wife of a prominent garment manufacturer who suspected that her husband was carrying on with one of his pretty young models.

Accordingly, she went to a detective agency with her problem. The agency took the job. They put their best investigator to work, and within a week the talented sleuth discovered that the wife's suspicions were well-founded. Hubby was very sweet on a cute blonde model.

"I'll get him," the wife told the head of the detective agency. "How much would it cost to get concrete evidence—enough to sue?"

The agency chief made a few notes on his pad. "With one investigator, a photographer and a witness, it will come out to $500."

The wife nodded. "Get started right away! I think I can borrow that much from my boy-friend."

☺

A.D. Frank, of Topaze Frocks, knows a manufacturer who recently interviewed a model for a job in his show room. He asked the girl about her experience, background and measurements. When the interview was completed, the fellow thanked her for her interest and said, "Where can I get hold of you?"

"I don't know," she answered, "I'm awfully ticklish."

☺

A wolfish manufacturer, who was sweet on one of his pretty young models, couldn't get to first base with her.

Finally, in desperation, he called her into his private office. "Ruth," he asked her. "Why do you spurn my love? Is it that you find me unfriendly?"

"Oh, no" she admitted. "I like you, Mr. Gold, but I have a boy-friend and I love him very much."

With that, the manufacturer walked over to a huge closet and pulled it open. "Look in this closet," he told her. "Do you see all those expensive hand-painted ties? Does your boy-friend have any of those?"

"No."

"And do you see those imported shoes? They're all hand-stitched. Does your boy-friend have any of those?"

"Well, no," she admitted.

"And those shirts," he said, pointing to a stack of expensive, monogrammed shirts. "Does your boy-friend have any like them?"

"No."

"Well, what the devil does he have?" barked the boss.

"He's got sex appeal," the girl barked back, "and I'd like to see you find that in your closet!"

☺

Johnny Frumkes, who manufactures coats, was talking to his brother Joe when an extremely striking model walked by.

"That's a nice dress you're wearing," complimented Joe.

"I change my clothes three times a day if the occasion demands it," said the model.

"Oh that's nothing," replied Johnny, "my sister changes 10 times a day."

"Ten times a day! How old is she?"

"Six months."

☺

Two catty models met in a show room. The first was of the ultra-thin fashion school, while the second was the full-blown, buxom type.

"To look at you, one would think there was a famine in America," said the buxom one.

"And to look at you," the thin one retorted, "one would think you were the cause of it!"

☺

Oriole Elias, of Royal Frocks, laughed when I told him this one:

An extremely attractive model appeared to be the perfect choice to display the manufacturer's new spring line.

"Yes, you're just what we need," he told her. "You have the right face, the right figure . . . everything my models must possess. By the way how much do you expect a week?"

The girl told him her figure.

"Sorry," said the boss quickly, "you're too tall!"

☺

Boss: Whisper the three little words which will make me walk on air.

Model: Go hang yourself!

☺

Alfred and Eliot Oshins, of Sportlanc Deb, were talking over business when one of their models walked in. She was a pretty girl, but on this occasion she looked very unhappy.

"What's wrong, Helen?" asked Eliot.

"You're looking at the dumbest girl who ever lived."

"Why do you say that?" asked Al.

"It's this way," began Helen. "I was on the way home from work yesterday when this Cadillac convertible pulls up alongside me."

"What happened then?" asked Al.

"Well, this tall young fellow in the car whistles at me."

"Yeah."

"I told him, 'I'm a lady, get out of here before I call a cop.'"

"Did that scare him off?"

"No. He tells me he'll take me to the best clubs in town and the finest restaurants. He says he's got a lot of money and he's lonesome. Then he says, if I don't want to do anything tonight, all I have to do is give him my phone number and he'll call me tomorrow."

"And what did you do?" asked the brothers Oshins.

"What could I do? I wrote the number down, and when I gave it to him he pressed something into my hand and drove away."

"Then what are you feeling so low about?"

"Because," wailed Helen, "what he put in my hand was a hundred-dollar bill! And like an idiot, I gave him the wrong number!"

Red Ruster and Jack Kay of Sandra Sage Fashions knew a model who was the vainest one of them all. When one was in the presence of this girl, he could never get a word in edgewise.

All she would talk about was herself. One day, however, she met a salesman, a handsome young fellow, whom she liked very much.

"Remember, dear," a friend told her, "men like to talk about themselves. If you don't let him say anything all night, he'll be bored and you'll lose him."

The model took her friend's advice. That night after she had spent three hours talking about herself, she asked, "And what do *you* think about my dress?"

☺

A salesman has to be many things. He must be a diplomat, a psychologist, a good speaker and even more important, a good listener. He must show a sincere interest in his product. But perhaps the most important thing a salesman must have is a repertoire of stories and the ability to tell them. For a salesman without a good collection of stories has handcuffs on his order book.

☺

Public Relations and advertising man, David Green, tells of the salesman who had just obtained a new position. One day while he was on the elevator with his new employer, the boss asked, "By the way, Morris, why did you leave your last job with Goldstein and Goldberg?"

"Well," explained Morris, "they were always arguing and I just couldn't take any more of it."

"Arguing?"

"Yeah, when Goldstein and I weren't arguing, Goldberg and I were."

☺

The brothers Lackritz—Harry, Joe and Sam--like the one I told them about the traveling salesman who arrived at a small town hotel one evening without any luggage.

"Where are your bags, sir?" asked the girl behind the desk.

"I don't have any," he replied.

"But you're a salesman and salesmen always carry samples with them."

"That's true in most cases, Miss, but not in mine, because I sell brains."

"I can't get over it," she exclaimed. "You know you're the first salesman I ever saw without samples."

☺

My brother Phil, who is sales manager for Forge Mills, and a great comedian in his own right, knew a salesman who had been on the road for more than six months. The fellow was the sentimental type and when he got back to the city, he decided to get a record of his girl's favorite song. Accordingly, he called a record store, or at least he *thought* he had dialed the store.

"Have you got 'Ten Baby Fingers And Ten Baby Toes'?" he asked the voice at the other end of the phone.

"No," came the reply, "but I have 18 kids in Alabama."

"Is that a record?" asked the salesman.

"I don't think so, but it's sure above the average."

☺

Phil's boss, Mal Malvin, told me about a salesman who had car trouble on a back country road. He opened the hood and inspected the engine.

"The trouble is in the battery," came a voice from behind him.

The salesman turned around quickly to see who had spoken, and the only thing in sight was a sway-backed old horse watching him over the pasture fence. Naturally, this completely unnerved the fellow, and he took off down the road. About twenty minutes later, he came to a filling station. After he caught his breath, he told his story to the owner.

34

"You mean to say that you saw no one near the car but that horse?" asked the garageman.

"That's right."

"Was it by any chance a black horse, sway-backed with bow-legs?"

"Yeah, that's right."

"Oh don't mind him," said the gas pumper. "He doesn't know a thing about engine trouble."

Cye Martin, of Stage Clothes, loves the one about the tie salesman who walked into the busy executive's office.

"How about buying some ties?"

"Don't need any. Scram!"

"They're pure silk."

"I said beat it."

"Look at these beautiful linings."

His patience exhausted, the big wig picked up the salesman and tossed him outside. Sample cases were scattered all over the place. Picking up his wares, the salesman brushed off his clothes, and walked back into the executive's office. "Now that you've got that off your chest, I'm ready to take down your order."

Advertising and P.R. man Charles Schlaifer knew a salesman whose hobby was entomology. His dream was to take a trip to Africa in order to hunt down rare specimens. Finally, he found the time and cash to realize his dream.

Making his way through the jungles of darkest Africa, he was surprised to come upon a small village and astonished when he ran into his old friend Benjamin Gross who'd been missing some months from the Garment Center.

"Benny, old pal," he cried, "what are you doing here?"

"I'm a witch doctor," explained Benny. "But what are *you* doing here?"

"I'm looking for a certain bug to add to my collection."

With this, Benny ran to a tree, cupped a small bug in his hand, and brought it to his friend. "Is this the one?"

"No, that's not it."

Benny went to another tree and went through the same procedure.

"Sorry, Ben, that's not it, either."

Benny picked up a leaf that was crawling wtih insect life.

"No," said the entomologist sadly. "All of those are a dime a dozen. The one I'm looking for is very rare."

"Well, I guess I don't have it," shrugged Benny. "But thanks for letting me show you my line."

Two salesmen, one from St. Louis and the other from Chicago, went deer hunting in Pennsylvania. Arriving at the main hunting lodge in the area, they were dismayed to learn that there were no vacancies. However, since they'd traveled so far, they decided to go hunting anyway.

That evening, coming out of the dense woods, they knocked at the door of an isolated farmhouse and asked the woman if she would be willing to put them up for a week. Although she was a widow and all alone, she agreed.

About six months later the businessman from St. Louis telephoned his friend in Chicago.

"George, I just received a wire from an attorney in Pennsylvania, and frankly I'm puzzled."

"Yes?"

"By any chance did you have an affair with that farm widow?"

"Well, look, Steve, I meant to explain that to you."

"And also, did you happen to give my name to her?"

"Well, er, I meant to explain that, too."

"Well, don't bother. The widow died and willed her farm to me."

☺

A salesman's relatives gathered for the reading of his will after his death.

"Being of sound mind," read his lawyer, "I spent every last cent before I died."

☺

The salesman had had a tiring day. He was glad that it was near closing time and hoped that he wouldn't have to wait on anybody else. But no sooner had the hope been formulated than a woman customer appeared at his counter.

"Do you sell men's bathrobes?" she inquired.

He told her that he did and took a couple of boxes off the shelf. Neither was appropriate. He took down two more. They weren't right either.

And so it went until the counter was strewn with boxes, tissue paper, and bathrobes of every color and description. Just as the harried salesman was about to reach for the last box, the woman remarked airily, "Oh, well, I wasn't planning on buying anything anyway. I'm just looking for a friend."

The salesman, whose back was turned, stopped dead. He turned around slowly and faced her for a long moment. Finally he said sweetly, "Madam, I'll take the last box down on one condition."

"Yes," she asked, wide-eyed.

"If you can give me any reason to believe," he exploded, "that your friend is in it!"

☺

A girl was telling her friend that she'd just become engaged to a traveling salesman.

"What's he like?" asked her friend eagerly. "Is he good-looking?"

"I wouldn't say he's handsome, just passable."

"Does he have a good personality?"

"He'd never stand out in a crowd."

"Does he have money?"

"If he does, he won't spend it."

"Does he have any bad habits?"

"Well, he drinks an awful lot."

"Lord, girl, if you can't say anything *for* him, why ever are you marrying the guy?"

"He's on the road all the time. *I'll* never see him!"

☺

Joe Marsh, of the Spindletop Restaurant, loves this one:

The salesman stood sadly at the front door of the farmhouse.

"I hate to tell you this, ma'am," he said, "but I just ran over your cat. I'm terribly sorry and I would like to replace him."

"Well, don't just stand there!" she snapped. "There's a mouse in the kitchen!"

☺

My brother Milton, of Kay-Windsor, loves this one:

It was a brutal night. The rain was coming down in sheets. The wind was blowing fiercely and visibility was almost nil. The salesman was having trouble driving.

"This is a rough one," he told his pet dog, Fido, who accompanied him on all his trips. "Looks like we're in for it!"

But no sooner had he stopped speaking than he spotted a small motel by the side of the road. He couldn't have been happier. He drove up and parked in front of the office, picked up his pup and walked in.

"I'd like a room for tonight," he told the proprietor.

"Sorry, mister," said the man at the desk. "We're all filled up."

"I could sleep on the sofa," suggested the salesman.

"That's where I sleep."

"But you can't turn me out on a night like this," protested the salesman.

The man at the desk simply shrugged, and the salesman realized it was useless to plead. He turned to go, but the proprietor stopped him before he got to the door.

"Just a minute, mister," he said. "Leave the pup here. I wouldn't turn a dog out on a night like this!"

☺

Since Bill Fine was a traveling salesman, he was forced to spend a large portion of time away from home. This might have made him the envy of some married men, but Bill was married to a remarkably beautiful girl—a statuesque blonde, flawless of face and figure.

No one could blame Bill for worrying about his wife when he had to leave her alone so much. What's more, he had reason to be jealous. There was evidence that she was not alone when she was alone. Suspecting, and not knowing, was driving him crazy and during one of his stopovers at home he hired a private detective to follow her while he was away on his next trip.

When he returned, he immediately called the private eye. "Tell me the truth," he begged. "Were my suspicions well-founded? I've got to know! It's the element of doubt that's driving me out of my mind."

"Well," began the detective, "it looks bad. As soon as you left the house, a tall, handsome guy went to the door. In a few minutes your wife came out and the two of them got into a car. I followed them in mine. They went to a night club and I went in behind them. I watched them dance cheek to cheek and hold hands at the table.

"After about three hours, they drove back to your house. Again I followed them and watched through the window. I saw them walk into the bedroom and embrace, but then they turned out the lights and I couldn't see any more."

"What did I tell you!" cried the salesman. "That element of doubt again!"

☺

Meyer Robinson, of Manischewitz Wine, knew two salesman who went wild game hunting in darkest Africa. While they were walking, they came to a clearing in the jungle.

Suddenly Jack whispered to Milton, who was directly in front of him. "Don't t-t-turn around t-t-too quickly, but is that a lion behind me?"

"You're asking me?" retorted Milton. "Am I a fur salesman?"

☺

Al the cutter was eating lunch with a salesman friend. Al ordered chicken noodle soup and his friend ordered borscht. When the waiter returned, he brought Al his bowl of chicken

noodle, but instead of borscht, he brought Al's friend a bowl of potato soup.

"I don't got borscht," the waiter told the fellow. "I brought you a bowl of potato soup instead. Taste it—it's very good."

He did and immediately his face lit up. "It's great. The best I ever had!"

Then he let Al taste it.

"It is good," Al agreed. "Waiter, why didn't you bring *me* some potato soup since it's so good?"

The waiter shrugged, "Did you order borscht?"

☺

Max Asnas, of the Stage Delicatessen, says, "Clothes don't make the man . . . but a good suit made many a lawyer."

☺

A salesman took a girl driving along a lonely country road. They came to a quiet spot and the car stopped.

"I guess we're out of gas," the salesman leered.

With this announcement, the girl carefully opened her purse and pulled out a bottle.

"Wow!" exclaimed the salesman. "You've got a whole fifth! What kind is it?"

"Esso regular," replied the girl.

☺

Irving Stempel, of McKettrick Williams, recently went to a baseball game with two of his friends. One was a sales manager and the other was the star salesman of the same firm.

At the game the salesman bet his boss that the Yankees would win. His boss picked Cleveland. The final score was New York, 5—Cleveland, 3.

"Thanks, boss," the salesman smiled as he was handed the $25 they had bet. "You know what I'm going to do with this money? I'm going to frame it so I can always show people I'm smarter than my boss."

"In that case," said the sales manager, "give me back the $25 and I'll give you a check."

Irving Nelson and Carl Rosen, of Puritan Dresses, prefer the story about the salesman who had tried unsuccessfully for five years to sell a tough prospect. After each visit, the salesman grunted, "I wish I had a hundred like you."

When the customer became curious and asked him why he kept repeating that phrase, the salesman replied, "I have a thousand like you, but I wish I only had a hundred!"

AND BEFORE WE LEAVE THE GARMENT CENTER
REMEMBER WHAT CONFUCIUS COHEN SAYS:
FAVORITE SLOGAN OF
PEOPLE IN THIS INDUSTRY IS
"PIECE GOODS ON EARTH
GOOD WOOL TOWARDS MEN"

COMEDY
AT THE COPA

Almost every comedian begins his act with, "A funny thing happened to me on the way to the theatre . . ." Well, nothing at all ever happened to me till I met Jules Podell, the famed impresario of the Copa.

In the many years I've known Jolly Jules, we've always been great friends on and off the job. Like his club, his home is fabulous and decorated in the best of taste. He must have spent a fortune just for the decorator's thought waves. I'll never forget the first time I visited him there.

Right away I noticed that he had pictures of comedians scattered all over the place. See what I mean about good taste? He has a terrific picture of Joe E. Lewis in his living room, a vivid (what else?) profile of Jimmy Durante in his study, and a striking oil painting of Danny Thomas in his bedroom. I can't tell you where my picture is . . . but every time I went to wash my hands, I saw it.

Seriously, though, the Copa is one of my favorite night spots. It better be. It's buttered a lot of my bread. And as a New

Yorker, I get a big kick out of entertaining the home folk, especially the wandering salesmen who are there in droves every opening night to cheer me on. In honor of this fraternity, many of whom make the Copa their home away from home, and office away from office, it seems only fitting that I should kick off with the one about the Knight of the Road who . . .

. . . was riding down an old dirt road when his car jerked convulsively to a stop. Looking around, he saw an old house, not fifty feet from where he broke down. He walked over and spotted an old farmer sitting on a rocking chair on the porch.

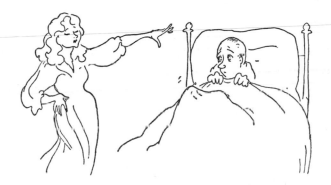

"Could you tell me where the nearest garage is?"

"It's closed for the night," the farmer informed him, "but you can stay here and I'll take you there in the mornin'."

That night while the salesman was fast asleep, he heard a loud knock on the door.

"Who's there?" he asked.

"It's only me," came a sweet voice from the hallway.

Then, before he could say another word, a beautiful blonde dressed in a revealing negligee entered the room.

"I'm the farmer's daughter," she cooed.

"W-w—well, what do you want?" he stammered.

"Don't you know?"

With this, the salesman jumped up, pulled on his pants, whipped on his shirt and bellowed, "I'm getting out of here!"

Amazed, the lovely lass called after him as he tore out of the room, "Brother, are you in the wrong joke!"

☺

Another salesman I knew wasn't so naive. Returning home after a long trip on the road, he immediately went to see his girl-friend.

As luck would have it, her little brother was seated in front of the TV set watching his favorite western program.

Annoyed by the little brat's presence, the guy decided to use some child psychology on him.

"Bobby," he suggested, "look outside the window and for every man you see wearing a red hat, I'll give you fifty cents."

"Sounds great," answered the little terror. Then he ran upstairs to look out the window.

Not ten minutes later, while the salesman and his girl were just getting reacquainted, the youngster suddenly dashed into the room.

"Didn't I tell you to watch for men with red hats!" shouted the irate salesman.

"But I did," the boy explained, "and while you were talking to my sister, a Shriner's Parade passed by. You owe me twelve hundred bucks!"

☺

However, there are many others who can justifiably point to money—or the lack of it—as the root of all their miseries.

I'm thinking specifically of a one-time prosperous manufacturer who had gotten himself into quite a predicament. He had run up large bills with three piece-goods firms, and all three were literally howling for his scalp.

In desperation, the manufacturer consulted his attorney. "Let's notify the newspapers that you've committed suicide," suggested the lawyer. "After that we'll hold a mock funeral, and if we carry it off convincingly enough, it'll solve all your problems."

It was an impressive funeral. Flowers were generously spread throughout the chapel and the house was good. At the proper time, everyone walked solemnly around the bier, and bid a final farewell to the deceased.

Then it was the three creditors' turn.

"Poor Irving," sighed the first. "He never paid his bills on time, but I'll sure miss him."

"S'long, Irving," said the second man, "too bad it had to end this way."

But the third creditor was enraged. "You louse," he snarled, "Pulling a fast one to get out of paying your bills! Even though you're dead, I'm going to get personal satisfaction!"

With that, he pulled out a revolver from his coat pocket and aimed it at the prone figure.

"Look, don't get excited," cried the corpse, sitting up. "You I'll pay!"

During one of my engagements at the Copa, Ed Sullivan phoned and asked me if I'd like to appear on his program. Naturally I was flattered and accepted his invitation.

The next day when I arrived at the studio to begin rehearsals and I saw Ed, I thought he was sick . . . he was smiling. While I was waiting to begin my act, I thought I'd cheer him up, so I told him this story:

After ten hectic years of marriage a battling couple had the worst spat of their marriage. Every piece of china was broken and

47

the house was a shambles. Thoroughly disgusted, the husband grabbed his hat and coat and stormed out of the house.

Not knowing where to go to cool his ire, the steaming spouse took the subway to Grand Central. When he arrived in the center of town, he decided that a visit to some of the local bars would make him forget his troubles. He marched into the nearest one and started downing highballs.

A few minutes later he emerged from the gin mill slightly besotted. He imbibed the fresh night air, and after a short walk, entered another bar.

By 3 A.M., the hapless husband decided that he had gotten up enough courage to take anything his wife could mete out.

He left the bar and started walking up Eighth Avenue looking for the nearest subway station.

Suddenly, he found himself in front of Madison Square Garden. He looked up and there in bright neon lights glared the sign: BIG FIGHT TONIGHT. He paused, re-focussed his eyes, and sighed:

"Home at last!"

Everyone who has ever been associated with the garment industry knows that almost every manufacturer employs beautiful, shapely models to display his latest fashions. Most of the buyers and salesmen they come in contact with are men, and being men, it is only natural that they appreciate how attractive these girls are. Models, of course, have to learn to be diplomatic in dealing with wolves. A show of outraged virtue, after all, could seriously hamper their careers.

Take the case of the two models who were discussing an out-of-town buyer who was dating one of them.

FIRST MODEL: I have a date with Sam.

SECOND MODEL: He's a wolf. He'll tear your dress off.

First Model: Thanks for telling me. . . . I'll wear an old dress.

☺

All models must be mindful of their appearance, and a few are especially vain. I'm thinking of one girl in particular—a very self-conscious lass, and I don't mean that she lacked poise.

Dress manufacturer Mike Levine swears he heard this from someone who heard it from someone who heard it from the model herself.

She had just entered her dressing room to change for her next stroll in a fashion show when she spied an elderly window washer working on the other side of the glass.

She had plenty of time so she decided to indulge in a little teasing. First she loosened one strap and let it fall from her shoulder. Then she loosened the other. She watched the window washer out of the corner of her eye.

No reaction.

Surprised and irritated, she wriggled out of the dress and slowly began to remove her slip, all the while keeping her eye on the old man behind the window.

Still no reaction.

"I'll teach you a lesson, you old goat," she muttered to herself. Quickly, she stripped off her remaining garments and walked boldly over to the window. She stood directly in front of the old man and glared at him.

He continued with his work, glancing at her blankly now and then. Finally, he stopped.

"What's the matter, lady?" he asked. "Haven't you ever seen a window washer before?"

☺

Bosses are another big source of conversation in the Garment Center. But, of course, it's nothing like the old days. Now that unions are here, a modern boss who wants to pull the wool over his employees' eyes, needs a much better yarn. Employees are independent and are not afraid to speak up for their rights.

This could be typified by the recent conversation between a cutter and his boss.

"You're nothing but a *capitalist!*" shouted the disgruntled employee.

"A *capitalist!*" screamed his boss. "Listen to me, Hymie. When I have a good season, I make money. When I make money, I pay taxes. When I pay taxes, I'm broke. When I'm broke, I have no money. When I have no money, I'm a bum . . . and a bum, *you* call a *capitalist!*"

☺

Every time I'm at the Copa, I always make sure that I get to see my old friend Leonard Lyons, the *New York Post* columnist. Besides being a terrific writer, Lenny has a wonderful sense of humor. Once while lunching in Lindy's, I told him this one:

An old waiter who had worked at Lindy's since it had opened, suddenly passed away.

Heartbroken, his wife, who had loved him dearly and had been very dependent upon him, didn't know what to do.

Then, as always happens in cases like these, she was swamped with advice from relatives and friends eager to help.

She was urged to see fortune tellers, spiritualists, magicians and cultists. She was told to attend seances where they communicate with the dead. But all these things proved disappointing, and she was getting progressively worse. Finally, her cousin, Irving, came up with a new solution.

"I've heard," he said, "that if you want to speak to a dead person, you have to go to the place where he spent most of his time."

Having tried everything else, the wife decided to go to Lindy's

and try out this theory. When she arrived there, she sat down at a table and started calling her husband. "Seymour," she asked, "can you hear me?"

"Of course I can hear you," came the low but clear reply.

"Seymour, can you speak louder?"

"No."

"Well then," motioned his wife, "come a little closer."

"Can't."

"Well, why not?"

"Because that's not my table!"

Phil Schwartz, of Red Cross Shoes, tells of the Copa chorus girl who, after seeing her name linked romantically with a noted romeo commented: "We have nothing in common. He's interested in girls and I'm interested in boys."

A lush hailed a cab outside the Copa. "Take me to the Copacabana, Driver," he shouted, as he hopped into the taxi.

The disgusted hackie got out and opened the door.

"You're in front of the Copa now, fellow," he snapped.

The inebriated character got out and glanced up at the awning of the nitery.

"Thash okay," he grumbled. "But next time don't drive so fast!"

☺

Whenever I'm at the Copa, I try to size up my audience and then tell the stories which I feel will amuse them most. However, there are many stories which are so universal that they amuse everyone.

For example, husband and wife jokes are always very popular with the customers. Because after all, every husband has a wife and vice versa. But marriage isn't the sacred institution it used to be. In fact, these days it seems that many a girl gets married just to keep herself occupied while she waits for the right man to come along. Just the other day, I heard two actors discussing the merits of a rising young starlet.

"Say what you want about her," said the first, "but before she's through that girl will probably make a good wife for five or six guys!"

Even more unbelievable was the conversation between the young movie queen and her fiancé: "Sweetheart, we'll have to postpone our marriage for a little while."

"But why?" he demanded. "Don't you love me?"

"Of course, darling. But I just married another man."

☺

But it seems that divorce is a luxury only for the rich. A poor man can't get divorced because he can't afford the alimony. You know what alimony is, don't you? It's the same as paying installments on your car—after the wreck.

☺

A Chicago housewife wanted to put her philandering husband in jail for not paying his alimony.

"Look," he pleaded, "I'll make it all up to you. We'll take a trip to New York. We'll take in the sights, see a show, have dinner, and then a few drinks in a nice little spot. Maybe we'll be able to rekindle the old flame."

His wife agreed. They took the train to New York and checked in at the Waldorf Astoria. Then they went out on the town. He took her to the Stork Club where they had some drinks and a steak dinner. Then they went to the Copa. When they left the Copa, the husband was so drunk that his wife had to help him back to the hotel and put him to bed.

When he was all tucked in, she began to worry about her children back in Chicago. Unable to sleep until she'd calmed her fears, she decided to call the maid long distance despite the lateness of the hour.

"Hello, Operator," she said, as she picked up the phone. "Get me Export 3-2333."

As soon as the drunken husband heard the phone number, he roused himself from his stupor, crying, "Hey, honey, don't call that number! It'll connect you with my wife!"

Furrier Sol Shulman told me this one:

He was a silk salesman and she was a buyer for one of the leading manufacturers. They met whenever he came to sell his latest items, and eventually he proposed. She accepted.

For their honeymoon, they went to Niagara Falls. They arrived on Friday night and had a wonderful time. Saturday and Sunday, too, were blissful days that he would never forget.

But when he awoke on Monday morning, she was gone. He quickly dressed, ran downstairs and searched all over for her.

Not finding a trace of her, he packed his bags and took the next train back to New York.

First he went home, but she wasn't there. Then he went to his office and sat down, brooding over his fate.

"What's the matter, Sam?" asked one of his co-workers. "Why are you so blue?"

Heartbroken, Sam told him about the events of the last few hours.

"Don't worry," his friend reassured him, "you know she never sees salesmen on Mondays!"

☺

Secretaries never seem to please anyone. If they're good . . . then their bosses dislike them . . . and if they're bad, their bosses' wives dislike them.

Of course, most secretaries are competent, efficient workers and are above reproach. However, there are good and bad of every kind . . .

Take the case of the cutie who was transferred to the New York office of a large garment concern.

When she was introduced to the boss, he told her, "All right, Miss Stone, do exactly what you did at the Chicago office."

"Okay," she answered. "Kiss me!"

☺

An equally forward secretary went to an Atlantic City convention with her boss. At the hotel desk, he did his best to get separate rooms. However, he was informed that due to the convention, only one was available. As they took the elevator up to their room, the manufacturer sternly warned his secretary that once they got upstairs she was to keep her mind strictly on business. The girl agreed.

But, that night after the lights had been turned out, the secretary impulsively decided that she wouldn't be averse to a little play. "Yooo, hooo, Mr. Gold," she cooed.

"What is it?" growled her boss.

"Can I have more of the covers? I'm awfully chilly."

Angrily, the boss tossed the cover her way. There was quiet for another minute. Then she cooed again. "Mr. Gold, yooo-hooo."

"Now what is it?"

"Would you like to do me a big favor?" she asked seductively.

"What?"

"Would you get me a glass of water? I'm very thirsty.

There was a slight pause. The manufacturer turned toward her, asking softly, "Miss Blatz, how would you like to be Mrs. Gold for just tonight?"

Excitedly, the girl cuddled closer. "Oh, I'd just love that!"

"All right," he bellowed, "then go and get your own glass of water!"

MIAMI MIRTH

Miami is God's country . . . He's the only one who can afford it! It's the land of the palms . . . all open. It's got hotels and motels. Some motels are built so poorly that you can hear the lady next door changing her mind.

When you get to Miami . . . you'll know it. No matter how hot it is, the women who have them will be wearing their mink coats.

Pepi Einstein, Leonard Lyon's wonderful mother-in-law, tells of one Park Avenue society girl who arrived in Miami on a day in which the temperature had zoomed well over 100. As she

got out of her car, she was overcome by the heat and fainted. A crowd of concerned bystanders gathered around her.

"Get a glass of water!" shouted one.

"Get a doctor!" screamed another.

"Open up her mink!" yelled the third.

☺

The first time I was in Miami, I appeared at the Terrace Cafe, which was owned by Lou Walters. I have also appeared in the Eden Roc, the Fountainbleau, the Sans Souci and the Five O'Clock Club, when it was owned by Martha Raye.

Martha's a great gal, and it was fun working with her. She's got a terrific sense of humor and really broke me up when she told me this one:

Willie Gordon, a cutter from the Garment Center, had had a good season. His boss had given him a lot of overtime, and being the thrifty type, he was able to save enough money to realize a life-long dream—a trip to Miami.

Neither Willie nor his wife had ever been to a really fancy hotel and naturally they were a mite nervous about the whole thing. One thing that bothered them was when and how much to tip. But they consulted with friends who were more experienced and learned what was the appropriate amount or percentage for various services.

Determined to appear poised and worldly, they set off for the southern resort city. When they arrived, they checked in at the swank hotel at which they had reservations, went to their room, and began to unpack. They congratulated one another on the smooth way the tip to the bellboy had been handled.

When they had finished unpacking, they changed into their bathing suits and set off for the beach. Mrs. G. couldn't wait to compare the Florida ocean to the Jones Beach waters. She dashed into the surf immediately and began swimming out. She swam so far and so long, that when it came time for the return trip, she became fearful she'd never make shore.

In a panic she screamed, "Help! I'm drowning!"

The lifeguard, who had been watching her from his perch, dived in and pulled her to safety. He carried her to the blanket where Willie sat frozen with fear and deposited her limp form beside him.

"Better not try that again," he advised her.

She opened her eyes and pulled her husband close.

"Willie," she whispered into his ear, "how much do we tip?"

☺

Sales manager Fred Perlberg was seated in a Miami restaurant with two of his associates when the waiter stepped up to one of his companions and asked, "What'll you have?"

"I'll have a salmon sandwich on rye bread."

"What do you want salmon for?" scoffed the waiter. "Tuna fish is much better. And instead of rye, take whole wheat. It's healthier for you."

"Good," agreed Fred's friend, "make it tuna on whole wheat."

"And you?" the waiter asked as he turned to the second man.

"I'll have bacon and tomato on toast. And give me a cup of coffee."

"Ha," scoffed the waiter, "do you think bacon's so good for you? And coffee, all it does is keep you up at night. Why don't you take a nice roast beef sandwich with a cup of tea."

"All right. Make it roast beef on whole wheat with tea."

Then it was Fred's turn. "And what do you suggest?" he asked, turning to the waiter.

"Suggest!" barked the waiter. "Who has time to make suggestions?"

☺

Jean Suits, manager of the Sans Souci, was host to a salesman who was vacationing in Miami. The man had taken an expensive course at Arthur Murray's dance studio before he left New York and, as a result, he was the picture of grace on the dance floor. At the Charleston, which was experiencing a revival in popularity, he especially excelled.

The first night he was in Miami, he received a wire from the home office that an emergency had arisen which necessitated his return on the morning plane. Instead of sulking, he decided to make the best of his only night in Florida.

When he entered the hotel lobby that night, he spotted a curvaceous cutie seated there. He engaged her in conversation and then took her dancing.

As they danced the Charleston in mad abandon, he romanced her. "Look, Ruth," he gasped, "I really go for you in a big way. But I don't have much time. I have to be back in New York in the morning. Can't we speed things up between us?"

"What do you want from me!" She panted. "I'm dancing as fast as I can!"

Miami *Herald* columnist, Jack Kofoed, tells the one about the tourist who pulled up in front of the Eden Roc, handed his suitcase to the porter and announced: "I've come here to spend the winter."

The porter shook his head and replied, "You come to the wrong place. We don't have any winter here!"

And Herb Rau, of the Miami *Daily News,* counters this with the one about the Miami man who died and went to his final resting place.

When he arrived, he noticed the palm trees and bright sun

beating down on all the inhabitants. "Gee," he remarked, "heaven is just like Miami."

To which one fellow quickly replied, "This ain't heaven!"

☺

Variety's Florida representative, Larry Sollaway, loves this story:

Three elderly men were sitting in the lobby of the Sans Souci. To pass the time they were discussing the effects of old age on them.

The first man, age 73, said, "My hearing is going. People have to shout when they speak to me."

"That's pretty bad," agreed the second man, age 79, "but I think I'm worse off. My eyesight is beginning to fail me. When I walk down the stret, I can't make out the faces of my friends. Even worse, I can't tell a blonde from a redhead."

Then they both turned to the third man who was 93. "And what's your trouble, Max?" one asked.

"Well," he began, "my trouble is much worse than yours. The other day, I was at home with my wife. We had dinner and then some wine. Later I fell asleep on the sofa. When I awoke, I noticed that my wife had gone into the bedroom, and when I entered, she was asleep. Shaking her gently, I said, 'Move over, honey, and we'll have a little fun.'

" 'But,' she protested, 'We had a little fun only twenty minutes ago.' "

The old man tapped his forehead thoughtfully. "My problem, gentlemen," he sighed, "is that my memory is slipping."

☺

Once, while I was flying to Florida, I was accompanied by Paul Yampole, of Miss Jane Inc., on his way to Miami for a well-earned rest.

A wolf who was seated behind us tried to make a play for the pretty hostess.

Moving close to her he said, "How about stepping out, sweetie?"

"Why not?" replied the girl, and opened the door of the airliner for him.

☺

Buyer Sid Kay, of R. and K. Originals, and I were seated in the lobby of the Fountainbleau when we overheard a cynic and his friend having the following conversation:

"When someone builds a better mousetrap the world will beat a path to his door."

"Bunk," scoffed his companion, "when someone builds a better mousetrap . . . some rat will steal it!"

☺

Paul Bruun, of the Florida *Sun,* had a friend who came from a family of writers. His sister wrote books that no one would read. His brother wrote songs that no one would sing. His mother wrote plays that no one would see and his father wrote checks that no one would cash.

☺

Two of Harry Mufson's recent Eden Roc guests were a New York buyer and his wife. He was a Garment Center buyer who had courted and eventually fallen in love with a shapely advertising copywriter. They wanted to have a June wedding and a honeymoon at Miami's Eden Roc Hotel, but the ad agency where the bride worked was in the midst of a hectic promotion campaign and the head of the agency was reluctant to grant her a leave.

Luckily, however, the girl was able to induce a close friend, Susan Rose, an unemployed copywriter, to take over for her during her absence. Since Miss Rose was an exceptionally pretty girl, the male copywriters at the agency were satisfied with the substitution. And the bridal couple had their June wedding and honeymoon.

Some weeks later, while the bride was out of town visiting her ailing mother, the groom was invited to a party. As he entered the apartment, the hostess greeted him and in the course of introductions, who should he come upon but the very same Miss Rose.

As the hostess began introducing them to each other, the young husband stopped her—and the entire party as well—by declaring:

"Oh yes, I know Miss Rose. As a matter of fact, she substituted for my wife on our honeymoon!"

☺

Dave Schwartz, of Jonathan Logan, prefers this one:

After having an extremely profitable year, the wealthy dress manufacturer went to his Florida home.

While he was in Florida he met a buxom blonde beauty and immediately fell in love with her. Since he was somewhat older

than she, he knew that a little diplomacy and bribery were called for.

"Marry me," he told her, "and I'll buy you a new Cadillac convertible."

"I've got two already," she told him.

"How about a new diamond ring?" he offered.

"I've got a beautiful ring already," she said, lifting her hand and displaying a huge, shiny stone.

"I'll give you an exquisite mink coat."

"I've got a mink and a sable, too."

Confused, the manufacturer asked, "Well, what do you want?"

"Cash," she replied, "just cold, hard cash!"

"Sorry," came the reply, "that's one thing I can't get whole-sale!"

Whenever I entertain in Miami, my old pal, Herb Kelly, of the Miami *Daily News*, usually attends at least one of my shows. Not too long ago, I noted that Herb was particularly impressed with this one:

A young man, who had recently graduated from Harvard, started out with a large silk firm as a stockroom boy. He was a bright lad, and within six months was made a salesman. In another six months he was upped to sales manager and shortly afterwards to general manager.

A few days after his last promotion, he was summoned by the president of the firm, who explained that he would retire soon and would turn the presidency over to the newcomer.

Overwhelmed, the young man said, "Thanks."

"Thanks!" growled the president. "You've been with this firm only a year. Is that all you can think of to say?"

"Well," said the young man, "thanks a lot, Dad."

And then there's the one broker Adolphus Roggenberg, of Newburger, Loeb & Co., tells about the two garment manufacturers who were seated on the beach in Miami when an old Garment Center acquaintance passed by. "You see, Max, over there," said one to the other. "He must have had a bad year."

"How do you know?"

"Because he's staying at last year's hotel!"

☺

The Lerner Boys of Philadelphia's Celebrity Room knew a thrifty fellow who came to Miami for the first time. Having heard about the prices of rooms in the gay resort, he decided to check with the desk clerk of the hotel before he signed the register. He walked up to the clerk and asked, "How much is a room?"

"A dollar a day," came the business-like reply.

"A dollar a day! Why that's wonderful! I heard that it was so expensive down here and—"

"And if you'd like a double occupancy room," continued the clerk, "it'll cost you a dollar and a half a day."

"Wonderful! Wonderful!" exclaimed the tourist. "At these rates, I'll be able to stay here for a month."

"I doubt it," answered the clerk.

"Why not?"

"The place is on fire!"

☺

And Miami *Herald's* George Bourke tells the one about the silk salesman who was on the first rocket ship to the Moon.

When he arrived, he immediately began a tour of the places to see how the Moon men did things. During his travels he entered a huge factory and asked a Moon man what was manufactured there.

"This is a baby factory," explained the man from outer space. "Our babies come off an assembly line."

Then the salesman, who was amazed by this phenomenon, gave the Moon man a detailed description of how babies are conceived on Earth.

"What do you know!" exclaimed the listener. "That's just how we make automobiles up here!"

☺

Dr. William Hitzig, the great diagnostician, who has always cared for my aches and pains, advised a Madison Avenue sportsman to take his ailing wife to Miami. The warm weather, he felt, would do her good.

When they arrived in the tourist town, the wife took a turn for the worse and the husband had to employ a full-time nurse. It just so happened that the nurse was a raven-haired beauty and the sportsman took an immediate liking to her.

The couple remained in Florida throughout the winter and when May came, they returned to New York.

About two weeks after their return, the husband received a letter. As he read the contents, a worried look came over his face. His wife, noticing his gloom, asked what the trouble was.

"Oh," he shrugged, "it's really nothing serious."

"But you seem so worried," she replied. "Won't you tell me what's wrong? After all, as man and wife we should share our sorrows and our joys. We're a team, you and I. We must share responsibilities. So tell me, darling, what's troubling you?"

"Well," he began, "since you put it that way, this letter is from the nurse."

"Yes?"

"It seems she's learned that she's in trouble, and she blames . . . us!"

☺

Sammy Citron, of Barbara Dance Frocks, shares my Miami fans' enthusiasm for this one:

The bride greeted her husband with a big kiss when he returned home from work.

Anxious to please, she asked, "Had a hard day? I bet you're tired and hungry. How would you like a nice, thick steak with french fries, a big tossed salad and strawberry shortcake?"

"No, dear, let's just have dinner at home."

Professors don't have a monopoly on absent-mindedness, agent Johnny Pransky tells me. He knew a businessman who returned from his honeymoon in Miami and spent days going through his files to refresh his memory as to what his own business was all about. He came across names on his calendar that he couldn't place for the life of him. One, in particular, bothered him because it looked familiar. Fearing that the name might belong to a business contact he couldn't afford to neglect, he decided to phone the number and find out who the man was.

"Hello," he said, "I'm sorry to trouble you, but I ran across your name on my desk. Is there anything I'm supposed to do for you?"

"You have already have," answered the voice on the phone. I'm your wife's first husband."

AND BEFORE WE LEAVE MIAMI
REMEMBER WHAT CONFUCIUS COHEN SAYS:
A HONEYMOON IS WHAT MAN GOES ON
BEFORE WORKING FOR NEW BOSS.

THE
BEST FROM TEX

Have you ever been to Texas? Well, if you have, you know that it's nothing but miles and miles of miles and miles . . . and by the time you get around to seeing it . . . you're too old to enjoy it.

When I was in Texas, I played at the Statler Hilton and the Shamrock Hilton. Hilton, you know who he is. He's the guy who builds hotels all over the world. He's even got one in Egypt. In fact, he's so progressive that he's got his architects working on the plans for a hotel that's simply out of this world . . . the Mars Hilton.

Speaking about Hilton, I wonder if Houston columnist, Paul Hochuli was kidding when he told me the following story:

A big game hunter, who wanted to add to his already impressive collection of trophies, induced a native of darkest Africa to lead him into dangerous territory never before explored by man.

After trudging through swamps and jungles, they came to a clearing. Turning around to the big game hunter, the native announced, "Me go now."

"But you can't leave me here!" pleaded the hunter. "I'll never be able to find my way back."

"You no worry," assured the native, "just sit down here, and before you know it, Hilton come and build hotel around you!"

☺

Getting back to Texas . . . and there's a lot to get back to, Texans as a group are probably the proudest people in this country . . . and the richest, too.

In Texas, they celebrate three holidays: Sam Houston Day, The Alamo Day, and December 15—that's the day the new Cadillacs come out.

I know one Texan who has two Cadillacs—one for red lights, and the other for green ones. But his neighbor has outdone him. He has *four* Cadillacs—one for each direction.

Texas is also the place where the men proudly proclaim: "Remember the Alamo," while the women counter, "Remember the Alimony!"

☺

Judge Abraham Lincoln Marovitz tells about a Texas wife who was suing her mate on the grounds of mental cruelty. As luck would have it, the judge was a life-long friend of the soon-to-be-shedded spouse.

"You will pay your wife $1,000 a week in alimony," the judge informed his friend.

"But Judge," pleaded the husband, "have a heart." Then he went into a long dissertation about how he had helped the judge attain his present position. He reminded him of how he had loaned him his assignments in high school and helped him maintain high grades.

"Well, I guess we can lower it to $500 a week," reflected the judge.

"And remember how I helped you with your math problems and your chemistry course," his friend continued.

68

"Make it $350."

"I even loaned you money to pay your tuition in law school."

"Three hundred it is," declared the judge.

Still not satisfied, his friend added, "And even after you grad-

uated, I was the one who fixed you up with a date for the home-coming dance, with the girl who was later to become your wife."

"So it was you!" roared the judge. He pounded his gavel and growled, "Case closed at $1,000 a week."

☺

Texans are famous for their prosperity. And some of them go to ridiculous lengths to point it out. Like the man who couldn't find a parking space, so he bought downtown Dallas.

☺

Dallas columnist Tony Zoppi says that gold-digging girls are always seeking to latch on to wealthy Texans.

He cites the case of the ambitious playgirl who ambled into a Texas bar and walked over to a prosperous-looking chap seated at the bar. In no time at all, they were deeply engrossed in conversation. In the middle of it all, the playgirl asked huskily, "Pardon me, but how much did you say your name was?"

☺

Danton Walker, the New York *Daily News* columnist who's a whiz on every subject, told me about another Texan who hadn't been feeling well for some time.

The rich rancher went to see his doctor, and after a thorough examination, the physician told him, "My advice to you is to take a trip to France. A rest in that climate will do you a world of good."

"Why go there?" asked the Texan. "I'll just send for it!"

☺

A Bostonian and Texan met on a plane headed for New York. Naturally, the cowpoke steered the conversation around to his native state.

"There's no place like Texas," he boasted. "Even our heroes are the bravest men in the world. Did Boston ever have anyone to match Sam Houston?"

"Well," countered the easterner confidently, "you've heard of Paul Revere."

"Paul Revere?" repeated the Texan. "Isn't he the guy who had to run for help?"

☺

A pair of Texans were taking a train trip across their native state. During a stop, they went into the station diner for a bite. When they reboarded the train, they noticed that a city dude had got on and taken one of their seats.

"That's my seat, son," one of the cowboys told him.

"It *was* your seat," corrected the new passenger.

Without blinking an eye, the Texan whipped out his six-shooter and shot the dude between the eyes. The conductor and a pair of porters carried out the limp form.

"You know, Clem," the sharpshooter told his friend as he reholstered his gun, "it's people like that who give Texas a bad name."

Even Texas doctors believe that there is no place in the world like Texas. Consequently, they think Texans are better in every respect than men from other places.

Willie Kolmar, of Kolmar-Marcus, the fellow who sells me my suits and never pulls any wool over my eyes, tells the one about the salesman who was down in Texas putting over a big deal with Neiman-Marcus.

One night he left his overcoat in his hotel room and caught a terrible cold. Try as he would, he couldn't shake it. In desperation he went to see a doctor.

Once inside the office, the doctor told him to take off his shirt.

"Ha," sneered the medico as he took it off, "you call that a chest? Texan men have hair on their chests as thick as wool." Then the sawbones looked at his arms. "And you call those arms," the M.D. sneered. "Texan men have hair under their arms as thick as wool."

Then the salesman, who was almost reaching the boiling point, removed his trousers.

"You call those legs!" the Doc shouted. "Texan men have hair on their legs as thick as wool."

The salesman had had enough. "Look, Doc," he exploded, "I came here for an examination—not to knit a sweater!"

Texans have their troubles, though—at least this story Benny Papell tells proves that ranchers do.

The worried man called the vet. "I don't know what's the matter with my prize bull," he complained. "It's time for him to get together with the cows, but the listless critter hasn't made a move yet."

The vet said he'd be right over. And so he was, with a bag full of hormones, vitamins, and remedies designed to perk up bulls. He worked over the animal for an hour and assured the rancher he could expect results in 24 hours.

Two days later the cow man called the vet. He was not satisfied.

"Aren't you being a bit foolish?" asked the vet. "What did you expect—a calf overnight?"

"Look, Doc," said the rancher. "Last night I put him in the barn with two cows. The least I could expect was a couple of happy faces!"

☺

Ben Mankin knew a traveling salesman who was swept off his feet by one of those tall, torrid Dallas models when he was traveling through Texas. After a whirlwind courtship, they were married and set off for a lavish honeymoon in Europe. For a month they really lived it up.

Trouble was that the salesman, at 62, was not the man he once was, while his bride, at 23, was in full bloom. By the time they returned to the groom's home in Brooklyn, he was worn down and out.

The first morning after their arrival, the salesman found he didn't have the strength to rise from his bed. A doctor was called. He examined the patient and found him suffering from acute physical exhaustion. As he was jotting down a prescription, the bride sauntered into the bedroom. Naturally, the doctor took note of her beauty and youth.

"Doctor," the patient called weakly. "Don't leave without telling me what's the matter with me. Come here."

The doc walked over to the patient's bedside. "Tell me the truth," whispered the aging salesman hoarsely. "Am I underweight?"

"Not dangerously," replied the doc, with a glance at the energetic bride. "Just undersexed."

Golf courses are the same the world over. I know one pair of Texans who were in the midst of a hot game when they were forced to halt by two women who were conversing in front of the 8th hole. Since they were some distance away, one of the men was appointed to approach the gossipy pair and ask them to move away.

He came back in a few moments, his face brick red. "Hank," he advised his friend, "I reckon you'd better be the one to talk to them gals. One of 'em's my wife and the other one's my girlfriend."

"Okay, partner," agreed his pal. "I reckon I can do that all right."

He started off across the links, but got no farther than the first man had. He was mopping his brow when he returned to the side of his friend.

"Tarnation," he muttered. "Small world, isn't it?"

A Texas girl was telling her friend about her fiancé, an elderly Texan twenty years her senior.

"Jasper's a wonderful fellow," enthused the engaged girl. "I'm sure we'll be very happy."

"But he's so much older than you are," pointed out her friend. "He won't enjoy the same things you do."

"That's unimportant," insisted the betrothed. "I love Jasper for what he is—president of a bank!"

A Wall Street financier asked a Texas oil tycoon, "How's business holding up in your part of the world?"

"Son," drawled the oil man, "in Texas we do more business by accident than you do on Wall Street on purpose."

Top lawyer Moses Polakoff had a client, an automobile sales-man, who visited his cousin in Texas during a vacation. While there, he decided to combine business with pleasure.

"Ken," said the salesman to his relative, "you've got a big place here, and from all indications, you do all right. But every time I look at that broken-down jalopy of yours, I start wondering about you, and I bet a lot of other people do, too. A fellow with your holdings should be riding around in a new car."

The old farmer regarded his younger cousin thoughtfully. "Frank," he began, "I don't need a new car. That there old one takes me where I want to go. Besides, I'd rather spend that same money on a good cow."

"Now, wouldn't you look silly riding to town on a cow!" taunted the salesman.

"Reckon I would," agreed the farmer. "But not as foolish as I'd look milkin' a car."

☺

Funnyman Al Kelly says: "When you find a pair of boots on the floor with a big ten gallon hat on top of them, what have you got? . . . A Texan with all the hot air let out of him."

☺

The story is told of a quick-tempered Texan named Luke who was sentenced to twenty years in prison when he drilled a fellow full of lead during a poker game.

Of course, he was lonely in his solitary confinement—no one to talk to—no one to pass the time of day with. But one day, an ant crawled into his cell.

At first, Luke merely studied the actions of the ant, and then he discovered what scientists have always known—the ant is quite a remarkable little fellow: In fact, the ant is capable of almost anything.

And so, with the aid of a small matchstick, the prisoner set about experimenting with a few tricks for the ant. At the end of the year the ant could perform somersaults. At the end of five years the ant could do a back flip. At the end of ten years it could rear up and walk around on its two hind legs.

Time passed. Two more years, and the ant could walk five feet on two legs; one more, and it could hop; another, and it could waltz to a tune whistled by the prisoner.

Still Luke persisted with his little insect friend. He taught it to play hide and seek, obey commands, such as "trot-walk-dance-hop" all in sequence. And then, finally, the day came when the prisoner was released from jail.

With the ant in his pocket, Luke went out into the world, confident that his talented pet would make him a fortune. Accordingly, he stepped into a bar and ordered a drink. Then he put his little trained ant—the only one of its kind on the earth—on the bar and called the bartender.

"Bartender," he began proudly, "see this ant?"

The bartender took a look. "Oh," he said, "I'm sorry, sir!" And down came a huge, hairy paw with a splat.

☺

A New York man who was vacationing in Texas, hired an old western guide to take him on an overnight camping trip.

"That's rattlesnake country, you know," the old cowboy informed him.

"There's a cure for snakebites, isn't there?" inquired the tourist.

"Out here when we get bitten by snakes we drink a jug of whiskey."

"Isn't there any other cure?"

The westerner gave him a quizzical look and drawled, "Who cares, son? Who cares?"

☺

And then there was the Texan who was telling an easterner about the eating habits of the rough and ready Texas ranchers.

76

"A real meal consists of two jugs of liquor, a couple of thick juicy steaks and a hound dog."

"A hound dog? What's he for?"

"Tarnation!" bellowed the Texan, "Who the devil do you think is going to eat all that steak?"

☺

Did you hear about the Texan who received a statement from his bank pertaining to a check he had recently deposited. The note read: INSUFFICIENT FUNDS . . . NOT YOURS. OURS!

☺

No, all Texans are not wealthy. There was the poor Texas peddler who happened to be selling his wares in front of a house of ill repute when the police raided the place. Just for good measure, they arrested him, too.

The night court judge, notoriously intolerant of untruths, barked at the first girl, "Well, what do you have to say for yourself?"

The girl wept bitter tears and cried, "Your Honor, this is a miscarriage of justice. I'm not at all what you think I am."

"Oh?" asked the judge, "and what are you?"

"I'm a dressmaker, Your Honor."

The judge's brow darkened and he roared, "Lies are one thing I will not tolerate! Thirty days!"

The second girl, too, wept. "Your Honor," she whimpered, "I've been wrongly accused. I'm not at all like my friend. I'm a milliner."

The judge became nearly apoplectic and raged, "I will not stand untruths! Thirty days!"

The third girl before him took an entirely different tack. She faced him squarely and declared, "Your Honor, I might as well confess. I'm not a dressmaker or a milliner. I've led a wrong life

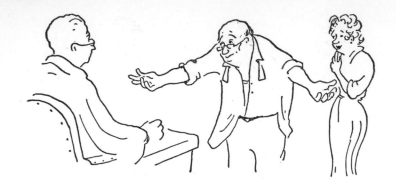

and I'm sorry for what I've done. Your Honor, I'm a street-walker."

A silence fell over the courtroom. Finally the judge nodded benignly and told the girl, "Young lady, your honesty must be rewarded. Sentence suspended."

The judge then glowered at the next case—the aged, wizened peddler—and snapped, "Well what's your story?"

The man stood up straight, bit his lip, faced the judge, and replied in a clear tone, "Your honor, I'm a streetwalker, too."

AND BEFORE WE LEAVE TEXAS

REMEMBER WHAT CONFUCIUS COHEN SAYS:

THE ONLY THING BIGGER THAN TEXAS IS TAXES

GAY AT THE CHEZ

Chicago is the Windy City. And when one goes to the midwestern metropolis, one can always separate the natives from the tourists. In Chicago, when the wind blows, visiting females hold onto their skirts. Hometown gals hold onto their hats.

☺

When I was in Chicago I appeared at the Chez Paree. The Chez is owned by Dave Halper. Dave is quite a wonderful guy and whenever we meet he greets me with a gag. During our last meeting he tossed this one at me:

A fire broke out in the girl's dressing room of a burlesque house. It took the firemen two hours to put the fire out . . . and it took three days to put the firemen out!

☺

Nate Gross, who writes the clever quips for the Chicago American, is another who loves to exchange funny ones with me. Recently Nate told me the one about the temperance lecturer who was telling the good people of Chicago about the evils of liquor. In no uncertain terms, he blasted John Barleycorn.

"Who has the most money to spend?" he bellowed. "Who has the biggest house? . . . the saloon keeper! Who has the finest fur coats and the most jewelry . . . the saloon keeper's wife! And who pays for all this? . . . You do, my friends, you do!"

A few days later, a couple who had been in the audience met the booze-baiter on the street and congratulated him on the wonderful speech.

"I'm pleased to see that you've given up drinking," the lecturer said.

"Well, not exactly," admitted the man. "We bought a saloon."

Charlie Dawn, also of the Chicago *American,* appreciated the one about the wife who told her friend, "I gave my husband a bottle of scotch, and he took it as an insult."

"So what did he do?" asked the friend.
"What could he do? He swallowed the insult!"

Agent Charles Rapp likes this one:
The dress manufacturer confronted his sales staff. "Which of you has been taking my model out after hours?"

"Boss," owned up one, "I didn't think you'd mind. I mean, I didn't mean any harm," but he was interrupted by the confession of another. So it went, each employee admitting that he, too, had not been immune to the charms of the model. Except for the youngest salesman.

"I'm happy to say," he announced self-righteously, "that I've indulged in no extracurricular activities with the young lady in question."

"You're just the man we're looking for," boomed the manufacturer. "Get right outside and fire her!"

Nat Sheinman, the dress manufacturer, swears that this happened in a Chicago dress house.

Every Friday was payday. Consequently, on that day there was more than $15,000 in the company safe.

During the lunch hour one Friday, the payroll clerk was alone in the office when two masked robbers entered.

"This is a stick-up," informed one of the pair, pointing a gun at the clerk. "Make a move and I'll drill you. Just open the safe and you won't get hurt."

Fearing for his life, the clerk obeyed, and the bandits scooped up all the money and put it in their pockets.

As they made for the door, the clerk shouted, "Just a minute!"

"Whadaya want?" barked one of the masked men, fixing his gun again on the clerk.

"Please take the payroll books, too! The auditors are coming tomorrow!"

Jack Eigen, the famed Chicago disc-jockey, tells of a housewife who complained to her husband, "Just look at me! My clothes are so shabby that if anyone came to the door they'd think I was the cook."

To which the husband retorted, "Not if they stayed for dinner!"

☺

Waiving economy, a young miss bought a new pair of shoes in the most fashionable and expensive shoe store in Chicago. After several days she returned to the store and complained that the shoes weren't comfortable.

"I just can't walk in these shoes," she groaned.

"Madam," said the manager haughtily, "people who have to walk don't buy shoes in this store!"

☺

Louis Zahn, of the Zahn Drug Co. in Chicago, admitted that this could have happened in his town:

The motorcycle cop was right behind the lady driver when it happened. She suddenly pulled over in front of the motorcycle, turned sharply, and he smacked right into her.

Cursing, the cop jumped off his cycle. "Why didn't you signal?" he demanded.

"Why should I?" she asked innocently. "I always turn off here!"

☺

Irv Kupcinet, of the Chicago *Sun-Times*, liked the one I told him about the wealthy New York dress manufacturer who died and tried to get into heaven.

"Who are you?" asked an assistant angel.

"I'm a dress manufacturer."

"Well, what have you done to deserve a place in heaven?"

"Why, just the other day, I saw a blind man on Times Square and gave him fifteen cents."

"Is that all?"

"Oh, no! Last week when I was walking on Riverside Drive I met a shoe shine boy who was half frozen to death. I gave him a dime."

"Is that in the records?" the assistant angel asked the bookkeeper.

The bookkeeper thumbed through the pages of his ledger and confirmed the claim.

"What else have you done?" continued the heavenly interrogator.

"Well, er—that's all I can think of."

"What do you think we ought to do with this guy?" the angel asked the bookkeeper.

"Give him back his quarter and tell him to go to hell!"

An imaginative member of a Chicago finance company sent the following letter to one of his delinquent accounts:

"Dear Sir:

"After checking our records, we note that we have done more for you than your mother did—we've carried you for fifteen months!"

Bentley Stegner, the Chicago *Sun-Times* scribe, roared at this one:

The tycoon barked, "Send the accountant into my office at once!"

The accountant, a young, debonair chap, stepped into his office. "You want to see me?"

"Now, listen here, you," began the big boss, "I will not tolerate your behavior a moment longer. A year ago you forged two checks in my name. Six months ago you sold our business secrets to a rival firm and three months ago you took advantage of my

83

daughter. Now the poor girl is going to have a baby. I'm warning you, the next least little thing you do—out you go!"

☺

Yes, this is a woman's world. When a man is born, the first question people ask is: "How is the mother?" When he marries, people say, "What a lovely bride!" And when he dies, they ask, "How much did he leave her?"

☺

Ann Marsters, the Chicago *American* columnist, tells of having lunch next to two young wives who were discussing the pitfalls of love and marriage. Ann couldn't help but overhear their conversation as they railed against their husbands and men in general. One of the chief complaints was the improvidence of their respective mates.

"If only I were the wife of a millionaire," moaned one.

"You mean, of course, if only you were the widow of a millionaire," corrected the other.

☺

Ira Arkin, of Ira L. Arkin Co., in the Windy City, loved this one:

Three old men were seated in Wrigley Field discussing their inevitable fate while they waited for the game to begin.

"When I die," said one, aged 76, "I want to be buried with John McGraw. He was a great manager and brilliant strategist."

"Me," said the second, aged 83, "I'd like to be buried with Abe Lincoln. Abe was a great man and all the people loved him."

"I," said the third, aged 92, "I'd like to be buried with Gina Lollobrigida."

"But she isn't dead yet," pointed out one of his companions.

"Neither am I!" cackled the old man. "Neither am I!"

☺

A husband was going about his usual daily routine on the morning of their 25th wedding anniversary, and his wife was rather peeved.

"Don't you know what day this is?" she scolded.

"Of course I do," he replied.

"Well, then, let's go to the Pump Room or something and celebrate. Let's do something unusual."

"All right," said her husband. "How about two minutes of silence?"

And if you're one of those who thinks that women do sometimes shut up, you'd do well to meet the fellow who would only go to a woman dentist. He claimed that it made him happy to hear a lady tell him to open his mouth instead of shut it.

And Jack Wasserman, the dress manufacturer, claims that the old theory that every woman has a price is *false*. He says he's never heard of a fellow who could find a buyer for his mother-in-law.

Which reminds me of the story Lee Sullivan, the Irish tenor,

told me about the big game hunter who went to Africa with his wife and his mother-in-law. They hired a guide and he took them on a safari into the wilds of the jungle.

One night, about a week after they were out, the husband and his wife awoke and discovered that Mama was missing. Naturally, they began searching for her. An hour later, they were shocked to see her cowering in a clearing with a huge lion standing over her.

"Oh, what are we going to do?" the horrified wife asked.

"Nothing," answered the husband quickly. "The lion got himself into that fix. Now let him get out of it!"

☺

A Chicago school teacher asked, "Billy, if your father borrowed two hundred dollars and promised to give his benefactor $10 a week, how much would he owe at the end of eight weeks?"

"Two hundred dollars," came the quick reply.

"I'm afraid you don't know your lesson very well," scolded the teacher.

"I may not know my lesson," answered Billy, "but I know my father!"

☺

And speaking about Billy's father, his wife recently brought him to court.

"Judge," she told the man on the bench, "my husband gets up every morning and immediately begins hitting me over the head with a frying pan. When he leaves for work, he punches me in the nose for good luck. Instead of eating lunch he kicks me in the teeth, and when he comes home at night he slugs me with a baseball bat and knocks me unconscious. Your honor, I think he should be put in jail for the rest of his life."

86

"Don't believe a word she says," said her husband. "She's punch drunk."

☺

Harry Katz, the Chicago packer, used to deal with a salesman who was quite a *bon vivant*. However, as he got older, the years of carousing began to take their toll, and he finally consulted a doctor.

"We can add thirty years to your life if you'll give up wine, women and song," the sawbones told him.

The salesman thought it over for a few minutes, and then said, "I'll settle for ten years, Doc. I never could carry a tune."

☺

Ed McGee, a native New Yorker, had married and moved to Chicago. The reason for his relocation: He wanted to be far away from his mother-in-law.

However, not two weeks after he moved into his new home, he walked in the front door and saw the old girl standing there surrounded by suitcases and trunks.

Naturally, he was taken aback, and while Mama was upstairs unpacking, the angry husband strode into the kitchen.

"As you know, my mother-in-law is here, and I've made out a list of her favorite dishes," he told the cook.

"I understand, sir," nodded the cook as she took the list from him.

"I'm afraid you don't," said Ed. "The first time you serve one of them . . . you're fired!"

☺

While eating at Carl's in Chicago, I overheard the fellow seated in the next booth call the waiter over.

"Why does this chicken have a leg missing?" he demanded.
"It was in a fight sir," kidded the waiter.
"Well then," cracked the diner, "take it back and bring me the winner."

And then there was the buyer from Marshall Fields who had this to say: "You never know where your next break is coming from. All you can do is pray that it won't be a compound fracture."

I knew one Chicago fellow who was so suspicious of his wife that when she gave birth to twins, he insisted that one looked like the iceman and the other looked like the milkman.

Judge Ben Shalleck tells of a colleague who once tried a case involving a traveling salesman who had sent his wife a telegram informing her that he was returning home to Chicago a day earlier than he'd originally planned. On his arrival, the salesman found her in a fond embrace with another man. Enraged, he tore out of the house, checked into a downtown hotel, and the next morning started divorce proceedings.

When the case came before the court, the judge asked, "Why do you want to divorce your wife?"

The salesman told him the whole story.

The judge turned to the wife. "Is this true?" he asked her.

"Yes, Your Honor," she admitted. "It's all true."

"In that case you ought to be ashamed of yourself!"

"But Judge! It wasn't my fault."

"What!" exclaimed the jurist. "How can you make such a ridiculous statement?"

"Can I help it if I never received the telegram?"

The subject of girls who love loosely reminds me of the Chicago "sporting house" that was raided. Inside, the police found a parrot, which they turned over to the local pet shop. The parrot was a garrulous old bird who swore a blue streak whenever it opened its mouth.

The pet shop owner finally sold it to a rich old society matron, who put the bird in a gorgeous cage, threw a cover over it and left it alone.

One night, about three weeks later, the matron had a big swanky party in her house attended by only the best people. When the affair was in full swing, the hostess suddenly decided to take the cover off Polly's cage. The old bird looked around, displaying a great deal of interest.

First he looked at the surroundings. "Brand new House" he croaked.

Then he looked at the woman. "Brand new women," cackled the parrot.

Then he looked at the men, "Ah—but the same old customers!"

☺

My old Garment Center pal Teddy Brown likes this one:

The pretty, but distraught, Chicago girl took her troubles to a psychiatrist.

"Doctor, you must help me," she pleaded. "It's got so every time a boy takes me out, I always end up saying 'yes.' And then afterwards I feel guilty and depressed all day long."

"I see," nodded the analyst. "And you want me to strengthen your will power."

"Heavens, no! exclaimed the disturbed girl. "I want you to weaken my conscience!"

☺

Diamond merchant Aaron Perkis knew a Chicago man who bought a farm out west. The ex-urbanite, however, wasn't much of a farmer and nearly all the heavy work fell to his wife.

For years he scarcely turned a hand. Finally his conscience caught up with him. One day, as he was napping next to the cook stove in the kitchen, he was roused by the entrance of his wife from the cellar. She was carrying a heavy load of coal.

"This has to stop," he cried. "For years I've been watching you carry that heavy load of coal up those stairs. From now on, there'll be no more of that, no sir! . . . I'm going to get you a smaller pail so you can make it in two trips!"

☺

AND BEFORE WE LEAVE CHICAGO
REMEMBER WHAT CONFUCIUS COHEN SAYS:
THE BEST WAY TO GET A JOB DONE
IS TO GIVE IT TO A BUSY MAN.
HE'LL HAVE HIS SECRETARY DO IT.

AMUSEMENT
IN ATLANTIC CITY

Atlantic City is the scene of the Miss America beauty contest. Every year ambitious beauties flock to this seashore resort with hopes of attaining fame and fortune.

Many of these girls are very publicity minded. I knew one Miss America aspirant, for instance, who was caught sun-bathing in her birthday suit by a brash photographer who promptly took her picture. The infuriated miss chased him all around the patio.

"I'll teach you to play a trick like that," she shrilled. "You shot the wrong profile!"

Or as one fellow I know puts it . . . a beach is a place where a girl goes when she has nothing to wear.

Bob and Harry, two enterprising young Garment Center salesmen who work the same side of the street, are an astonishing pair. Neither of them was remarkable as a single, but since they teamed up, their record has been unbelievable.

Skinny D'Amato, of the "500 Club" in Atlantic City, tells a story about the legendary duo which might explain their success.

91

They were at a convention in Atlantic City. Hoping to combine pleasure with business they were standing behind a pillar, casing the joint, when they spied a striking model posing languorously on a sofa not far off.

Bob, the handsomer of the pair, strolled over and introduced himself while Harry remained hidden behind a pillar.

In ten minutes Bob had maneuvered the curvaceous lass up to his room. Safe from the prying eyes in the thronged lobby, Bob took the girl in his arms and whispered, "How about a little kiss?"

The girl was willing, but she had to think of her obligations, too, so reluctantly she held out for ten dollars.

"All right," said Bob, "ten dollars it is, but on one condition."

"Yes?"

"That you let me turn out the lights and kiss you as many times as I want to and for as long as I want."

The girl agreed.

Two hours later, she whispered in his ear, "Gee, you're kissing better than ever, Bob."

"Bob's at the Turkish bath," chuckled Harry, "but he'll be taking over again in ten minutes."

☻

Murray Hamburger, who makes bridal gowns, tells the one about the garment salesman who was vacationing in Atlantic City with a colleague. During the vacation they spoke about many things, but inevitably the salesman got around to talking about his wife. "When I was first married," he began, "I was the happiest man in the world. When I came home at night my wife would get my slippers, and my dog would run around the room barking at me. And now, after ten years of married life, everything has changed. Now the dog brings me my slippers and it's my wife who runs around the room barking at me!"

"So what are you complaining about?" shrugged his friend. "You're still getting the same service."

☺

And David Mankin tells the one about the salesman who suspected his wife was running around with other men. Just to make sure, the fellow hired a private detective to tail his spouse.

A week later the Sherlock reported and said, "You were right. Your wife *is* running around with another man." Then he submitted his bill. "And what are my next instructions?" asked the detective.

"I want you to follow my wife and that bum. Keep on their trail night and day—even if you have to track them the length of Europe and back. And then I want a complete report on what he sees in her."

☺

Joe Leventhal, the dress manufacturer, is a good listener to a good gag. I cornered him recently and sprang this one on him:

Max was one of those men who was a born optimist. No matter what happened his philosophy would be: "It could've been worse."

One day a tragedy took place in the neighborhood. Ben, his next door neighbor, who was a traveling salesman and spent a good deal of his time away from home, returned unexpectedly one night and found his wife in the arms of another man. In a blind rage, Ben ran to a drawer, seized his pistol, and shot and killed both his wife and the stranger. The district attorney charged him with double murder.

Naturally, the whole neighborhood was abuzz with talk about the calamity. But every time the tragedy was discussed in Max's presence, he'd simply say: "Oh, well, it could've been worse."

"Are you crazy, Max?" one of the neighbors jumped on him. "What could possibly be worse? Two people are dead and a wonderful fellow like Ben will probably be executed!"

"Nevertheless, I still claim it could've been worse. If Ben had come home Wednesday instead of Thursday, you'd be sending *me* flowers."

☺

The aged salesman who had attended more than 50 Atlantic City Conventions left the dining room right after dinner. His younger associates had invited him to accompany them on some fun and frolic, but he refused. "I'm not as young as I used to be," he apologized. "I think I'll just turn in."

When he was upstairs, he undressed slowly and then crawled into bed. But no sooner had he turned off the light, than a gorgeous blonde model opened the door and slinked in.

Puzzled, the old salesman switched on the light and looked up at the dazzling damsel.

"Oh, I'm terribly sorry," said the girl," I guess I'm in the wrong room."

"Oh no," sighed the salesman, "you're in the right room—but you're about 40 years too late!"

☺

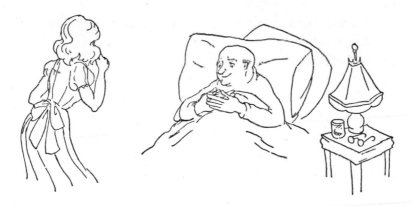

Sam Love tells of a publicity man who was showing a promoter around the new stage for the Miss America contest in Atlantic City. "That girl," he said pointing to one of the entrants, "is wearing a $15,000 bathing suit."

"That might be true," agreed the promoter eyeing her carefully, "but her heart isn't in it!"

☺

"Roast Beach is our favorite sport," the Atlantic City lad told his friend from New York.

"Roast Beach?" asked his pal, "why I never heard of that game. How do you play it?"

"Every day," explained the young native, "we go down to the beach and see who's cooking!"

☺

Nat and Billy Rolfe were recently in Atlantic City. One afternoon while they were seated in the lobby of their hotel waiting for dinner to be served, they overheard a fellow telling his friend the following story:

A prominent manufacturer of women's panties was a little hard-pressed for money. Accordingly, he went to the nearest bank to ask for a loan. He was given all sorts of papers and forms to fill out, and finally, one of the bank executives interviewed him.

Looking over the forms, the banking man glanced up at the panties man and said, "I don't know if you're a good risk. How many pairs of panties have you in stock right now?"

"One hundred thousand," answered the manufacturer.

The executive pulled out a pad, jotted down a few memos and then said, "Well, in that case I guess we can give you the money."

One week later, the manufacturer returned to the bank and handed the banker the money he had borrowed along with the interest. "I sold my panties and made a big profit," he said.

"Well, that sounds wonderful," enthused the banker. "Now that you have all that extra money, why don't you bank it here?"

"I'd like to, but first I'd like to ask you one question."

"Yes, go right ahead."

"How many panties do *you* have in stock?"

The Latin Quarter's Ed Rissman tells about a dress manufacturer who staged a fashion show in association with a Miss America Beauty Contest. In the middle of everything, he discovered that one of his top models had disappeared.

Frantic with worry, the manufacturer told one of his salesmen, "I've got to find a pretty girl to fill in for her."

"It just so happens," the salesman told him, "that I know a model who can replace her."

"Can you lay your hands on her?" cried the excited boss.

"I'll thank you to leave my private life out of this!" retorted the salesman.

The curvaceous cutie bounced into an Atlantic City bank and placed a check before the teller.

"Do you have an account here?" asked the man in the cage.

"No."

"Well, I'm afraid I can't cash your check then unless you can provide me with some sort of identification."

"I'll find someone to vouch for me," said the girl and flounced out of the building. In a minute she returned with a cop.

"Hello, Clancy," greeted the teller. "Do you know this woman?"

"I most certainly do!"

Reassured, the teller cashed the check and the girl departed with a fistful of greenbacks.

"I'm glad you were on the corner," the teller told Clancy. "I couldn't cash her check without some sort of identification."

The policeman scratched his head thoughtfully. "Let's see, it's goin' on fifteen years Gert's been makin' the conventions here," he calculated. "That is, not countin' them three years in stir on that bad check charge. . . ."

☺

Joey Gold & Jesse Berley were describing one of their unpopular associates to me.

"He's the kind of fellow," mused Joey, "who throws a drowning man both ends of a rope."

☺

Nat Tuman tells of the two old school pals who were seated in an Atlantic City bar reminiscing.

"I'll always remember my school days," said one, "I'd say they were the happiest days in my life."

As he was speaking he saw another fellow walk in to the bar.

"Charlie," he nudged his friend, "isn't that Mr. Berlin, our old principal?"

"It certainly looks a lot like him," agreed his associate, "but don't you think he'd be a little older?"

"Maybe not. He was a pretty young principal."

"Yeah, he was a real nice guy. I can't remember him ever so much as raising his voice. Everybody liked him."

"Why don't you go over and see if that's him?" suggested Charlie.

With this his friend walked over to the fellow and asked if he was their former principal.

"Why don't you get the hell out of here and stop bothering me," growled the man. "You got a lot of nerve!"

Unhappily, the fellow rejoined Charlie, "Now we'll never know if that's him," he said sadly.

☺

Will Steinman knew an elderly couple who went to Atlantic City on their 50th anniversary. They took a lavish suite overlooking the ocean so that they could watch the tides.

One afternoon while they were seated near the window, the wife poked her spouse in the ribs and said, "Look, Irving, there's a mermaid!"

The husband was unimpressed, "A mermaid—what's that?"

"You don't know what a mermaid is? It's half woman and half fish."

"So?"

"So, nothing—I bet you'd be interested if it were half herring!"

☺

Jimmy MacWhan, who handles special service for the Pennsylvania Railroad, likes this one:

The broke hobo approached the circus manager for a job. "What can you do?" the boss asked.

"I jump off a 50-foot tower and land in a tank of water five feet deep."

Impressed, the manager agreed to try out the act that night.

At eight sharp, the hobo was there. When the band began to play, he climbed to the top of the tower. Then, with the floodlights shining on him and the drums rolling, he dived into the tank.

The crowd went wild; and the manager, realizing he had a find, approached the daredevil. "You're great," he enthused. "I'm going to make you the star of the show. Can you sign a contract right now?"

"Nothing doing," replied the hobo. "Once is enough. A fellow could get himself hurt pulling a fool stunt like that."

☺

Returning home from Atlantic City, my dentist, Dr. Ira Landau, was stopped by a traffic cop.

"Can't you read, Bud?" asked the policeman sarcastically.

"Why, of course, officer."

"Well, you don't act it. The signs say 50 miles an hour and you were going 60."

"Sixty!" my dentist protested. "I wasn't even going 30!"

The officer merely glared.

"In fact," continued the doc, "I wasn't going 20, or even 10!"

So the officer gave him a ticket for illegal parking.

☺

A generous tipper at an Atlantic City hotel found a brand new waiter serving him one morning.

"Where's Charlie, my regular waiter?" he demanded.

"Well, I'll tell you," explained the new man, "Charlie got himself involved in a little crap game last night."

"Aha!" chuckled the patron indulgently. "He struck it rich and he's taking a little vacation, eh? I get it."

"I'm afraid you don't," continued the new waiter. "Charlie lost. *I* won . . . you!"

☺

AND BEFORE WE LEAVE ATLANTIC CITY
REMEMBER WHAT CONFUCIUS COHEN SAYS:
IN ATLANTIC CITY ONLY THING WORSE
THAN RAINING CATS AND DOGS
IS HAILING JITNEYS.

LAS
VEGAS
LAUGHS

Las Vegas is the place where they give you odds that you'll never get even.

In recent years, Las Vegas has become the gambling center of this country and the good citizens of that fair city have taken great pains to drive home this fact to visiting tourists.

Out in Las Vegas they have traffic lights that say—"STOP"—"GO" and "6 TO 5 YOU'LL NEVER MAKE IT." And all the motels have three types of towels: "His" . . . "Hers" and "You Wanna Bet!"

Las Vegas is a scenic town replete with many of the nicest hotels in the country. Some of the better hotels are "The Sands," "El Rancho Vegas," "The Thunderbird," "The Flamingo," "The Royal Nevada" and "The Dunes." The owners of these hotels are all wonderful people. They pay you your salary and then invite you to go into the gambling room and double it . . . or lose it.

They even have dice made from Ivory Soap so that you can have floating crap games in the swimming pools . . . and after you play . . . you're really washed up.

Yes, everyone in Las Vegas is betting conscious. I know one fellow who walked into a Las Vegas diner and ordered a plate of pancakes. When he got them, he looked them over and screamed to the waiter, "Take them back! They're marked!"

And once when I passed a funeral parlor, I noticed the undertaker standing outside his mortuary. "How's business?" I asked.

"Not too good," he answered sadly.

Peering inside, I noticed four coffins with bodies in them. "But, you have four customers," I said. "Don't you consider that a good day's work?"

"Only one," he corrected. "Three of them are shills!"

☺

Agent Mark Leddy says Las Vegas is the only place in the world where they play the show "You Bet Your Life" . . . for real.

Jack Entratter, the gay blade of The Sands, recently told me about a fellow who used to come to his hotel every night and beg the guests for money.

"Please," he'd ask anyone who would listen, "just loan me $100. I'll double it in no time and pay you right back."

But night after night, people would shake their heads and walk away. However, one night, he ran into a generous oil man from Texas who handed him a crisp C-note and told him, "Here, Boy, enjoy yourself!"

After thanking his generous benefactor, he walked over to the Black Jack table and blew the money in five minutes. The next night when he saw the Texan, he again asked him for some money, and again a hundred-dollar bill was forthcoming. But that, too, was gone within a matter of minutes.

This continued for more than three weeks. Every night the Texan would give him money, and every night it would be gone almost before he had it.

Finally, in desperation, the unhappy fellow told one of his friends about his experience with the generous Texan.

"There's only one thing to do," his friend told him. "Lose the bum—he's bad luck for you!"

☺

Frank Sinatra, who frequently entertains in Las Vegas, knew a young couple who went to the Nevada gambling town on their honeymoon.

Upon arriving at the resort town, the husband immediately became fascinated by the plush gambling rooms and started betting on all the attractions. And just four days after their arrival, as a result of continued bad luck, they had just $2 left between them.

"Let me go down to the gambling room alone," the husband told his wife. "I've got a feeling that today my luck will change."

Once downstairs, he walked over to the roulette table and put his last two dollars on number 14, black. Luckily, his number won. He continued betting and his luck was fabulous. Over and over again, his would be the winning number, and within one hour, he had run his winnings up to $50,000. Feeling that his luck was bound to change for the worse, he picked up his winnings and started walking toward the cashier's cage. But just before he reached it, he felt one final urge to bet. Taking his entire winnings, he walked back to the roulette table and placed it all on number 16, red.

The wheel began to spin round and round until it finally stopped on number 12, black. Heartbroken, the young fellow walked slowly to the elevator and went up to his room.

Upstairs, his wife, who was impatiently awaiting his return, asked anxiously, "Well, Harvey, how did you make out?"

"I lost the two dollars," he told her sadly.

And then there is the Joe E. Lewis story about the big gambler who went to Las Vegas to double his fortune. Checking into a hotel, the man wasted no time finding his way to the Black Jack tables.

But the gambler ran into a streak of bad luck, and in no time at all, lost all his money. Left without a penny to his name, the despondent chap decided to take his life.

He walked out of the gambling casino and looked for the nearest cliff. He was just about to jump when he heard a mysterious voice behind him say, "Don't jump off the cliff."

Startled, he asked, "Why not?"

"Go back to the casino, borrow two dollars, go over to the roulette wheel and bet on 10, black."

The fellow did as he was told. Naturally, he won. "Now bet on 12, red," the voice instructed.

And again he won. This went on for more than an hour. Each time he did as the voice told him, and each time he won. When he counted his winnings, he found that he had more than $25,000 in chips.

"Stop gambling now," the voice told him, "I can't help you any more."

But the fellow disregarded the advice and put his entire fortune on 11, black. The wheel spun around, and his number lost.

"Oh, I'm broke again," moaned the broken-hearted gambler. "What am I going to do now?"

"Jump off a cliff!" the voice from behind him said.

Las Vegas is the only town in the world where you get tanned and faded at the same time. But don't get me wrong, some people do make big killings in the gambler's paradise.

Two fellows I know were speaking about a friend of theirs who had just left Las Vegas with a bundle of money.

"Joe," said one, "left Las Vegas with $50,000."

"I know," said the other, "but he went there with $100,000!"

Talent representative Eddie Rio says Las Vegas is Monte Carlo with Cowboys. I heard about two westerners, who at the end of a particularly torrid card game, surprised each other by announcing, "I've got five aces!"

"Well then, who wins?" asked an onlooker.

"The one who draws first!"

☺

"In Las Vegas," says insurance man, Gerson Geizler, "people are always kind to animals . . . that's why they're always giving money to the kitty."

☺

Speaking about animals, Beldon Katleman, the shining light at El Rancho Vegas, likes the one about the Las Vegas bookmaker who was given a parrot in lieu of a cash payment by one of his clients. And to tell the truth, the parrot was truly a talented bird. Not only did he speak English perfectly, but French and Spanish as well.

Being a whimsical sort, the bookie took his bird with him one night when he went to "El Rancho."

While standing at the bar, the bookie got into a conversation with the bartender, and in a few moments was raving about his new bird.

Having heard such claims before, the bartender was not impressed. Irritated, the bookie offered to bet the bartender $50 that

his parrot could speak to him in three different languages. The bet was made quickly.

"*Parlez-vous français?*" said the bookie to the parrot.

There was no response.

Nor did the parrot respond to questions in English or Spanish, and the bartender pocketed the $50.

When they were outside, the bookie screamed at his bird, "What a stupid parrot you are! You just cost me $50 because you turned temperamental."

"Don't be a jerk," replied the parrot. "Just think of the odds you'll be able to get in that joint tomorrow!"

☺

Another of Beldon's favorites deals with the farmer who asked the clerk in the town sporting goods store to show him a shotgun.

Naturally, the clerk reached for the most expensive rifle in the place and handed it to him.

"This is our finest model," the man behind the counter told him. "Notice the craftsmanship. It's a bargain at $250."

"Oh, that's too expensive. What else have you got?"

Then the clerk took out another model and told him that it was a steal at $175.

"Too much," grunted the farmer, "I'd like to see another one."

The clerk took another weapon from the shelf. "This is the cheapest one we carry," he sneered, "no special features, factory produced. It costs $12."

"That'll be good enough," agreed the farmer. "After all, it's only a small wedding."

☺

Arranger and talent manager, Harry Brent, knew a couple who decided to take their second honeymoon in Las Vegas. The husband was a big card player and every night he made his way to the black jack tables. His wife always remained in the room.

One night, while he was in the midst of a hot game, a bell-hop came running over and hissed, "Mr. Fenton, your wife is upstairs making love to your best friend."

Enraged, the husband shouted at the dealer: "Hurry up and deal! This is positively my last hand!"

☺

Stan Irwin, the bright boy of the Sahara, recently received a letter from a fellow who asked Stan's advice about the best way to handle his landlord. Stan wrote the fellow and told him which would be the best course to follow.

Not one week later, Stan received the following reply:
"Stan:

"I wrote you about my troubles with my landlord. You advised me and I took your advice. Now I'm not having any more trouble with that dirty bum.

Sincerely,
JOE MUGG
Sing Sing Cell 110421"

☺

"How far is Reno?" a tourist asked a native of Virginia City, the headquarters of Café Society expatriate Lucius Beebe.

"Oh, it's 25,540 miles the way you're heading," the native told him, "but about 20 miles if you turn around!"

☺

Sophie Tucker, the grand old lady of show business who frequently appears at El Rancho Vegas, has a great sense of humor. Whenever we meet, I always spring the latest gags on her—I love to listen to that hearty laugh of hers.

Among her favorites is the one about Jack Goldberg, who left a small upstate New York town and came to New York to seek fame and fortune.

In his ten years in New York, Jack realized both his ambitions. He became a prominent member of the Garment Center and lived in a fashionable Fifth Avenue apartment.

One day, Jack got an uncontrollable urge to visit his old home town. He wanted to impress his friends with his great success and wealth.

The next morning, he was on the train. When it stopped at his birthplace, Jack picked up his suitcase and walked proudly through the depot. As he emerged from the depot, he was feeling a little disappointed, because he hadn't come across any of his old friends. But upon hitting the street, he was immediately stopped by Artie Flowers.

"Hey, Jack," shouted Artie, "what're you doing? Leaving town?"

Everyone who goes to Las Vegas isn't prosperous. Recently, while I was standing in the lobby of El Rancho Vegas, I spotted an odd-looking cowboy walking into the hotel.

Completely oblivious to everything going on around him, he strutted up to the desk and signed the register with a big "X."

The desk clerk noticed that the new guest had left muddy tracks clear across the new rug. "Sir," he admonished the cowboy, "when you patronize a hotel which prides itself on its cleanliness, you might at least wipe half the mud of Texas off your shoes."

The Texan eyed the room clerk with honest amazement and asked softly, "What shoes?"

While a guest on a small yacht cruising around Nevada's huge Lake Tahoe, a has-been movie actor accidentally slipped over the side. Immediately the crew went into action, sweeping the water with the ship's spotlight until it illuminated the figure of the actor. He was threshing about wildly—his stuntman had always done his swimming for him.

"Don't panic," admonished one of the crew. "We'll be with you in just a minute."

"Just throw me a life preserver," gurgled the actor, "and then take your time. It's been so long since I've been in the spotlight!"

Coat Manufacturer Willie Cornet overheard the following conversation in Las Vegas:

MARILYN: How can I have beautiful hands?

DIAMOND JIM: Deal yourself plenty of aces.

And there's "Music Man" Jack Kahner's favorite about the young couple who checked into a Las Vegas hotel. When the bellhop took them to their room, they nodded approval. The boy was given a generous tip, and as he was about to leave, he asked, "Will there be anything else, sir?"

"No thanks," said the man.

"Anything for your wife, sir?" the boy asked.

The man meditated for a moment, then looked up and said, "Why yes, come to think of it. Bring me a post card to send her."

☺

In Las Vegas, everything is wonderful:
You can't beat the weather . . .
You can't beat the hotels . . .
And you can't beat the crap tables!

☺

In the great gambling town, says Choreographer Boots McKenna, they have a drink called the Lottery Cocktail . . . one drink and BINGO!

☺

They were married in New York and went to Las Vegas for their honeymoon. They checked in at The Sands, and were having a wonderful time until their first spat three days later.

"I've had all I can take from you already!" threatened the disillusioned bride. "In fact, I'm through! I'm getting out of here. You'll be sorry when I become a big star. I'm going to Hollywood, or else back to New York—alone! I'll become a famous model or a big name in television. But wherever I go or whatever I do, I'm leaving you!"

With that, she marched out the door, slamming it angrily behind her. Hardly five minutes had passed before she was back.

"I thought you were leaving," said the bridegroom mildly.

She began to unpack huffily. "Lucky for you it was raining," said she.

☺

Jack Squire's favorite concerns a 92-year-old grandfather who returned from a Las Vegas vacation and announced to his family that he'd met his future wife.

"You! Married!" they exclaimed in unison. "Who is she? How old is she?"

"Her name is Sara Cohen," said Grandpa, "and she's 18."

"Eighteen!" repeated his grandson incredulously. "How can you consider marrying a girl of 18!"

"Why not?" asked Grandpa calmly. "She's exactly the same age as my first wife when I married her."

AND BEFORE WE LEAVE LAS VEGAS

REMEMBER WHAT CONFUCIUS COHEN SAYS:

THE ONLY WAY TO DOUBLE YOUR MONEY

IN LAS VEGAS

IS TO FOLD IT AND

PUT IT IN YOUR POCKET.

CATSKILL CAPERS

Ranging from Monticello to Liberty, the Catskills is one of the most popular resort areas in this country. When a proud patriot like Patrick Henry can say "GIVE ME LIBERTY OR GIVE ME DEATH!" and a great statesman like Thomas Jefferson confesses that he likes to: "SPEND MY SPARE TIME IN MONTICELLO," you just know that these places are something special.

The fellow who called the Catskills the Derma Road knew what he was talking about.

And if you're ever in the Catskills and you see a white line on the road . . . *Remember!* . . . that's not paint . . . it's *sour cream!*

I've played in the Catskills many times and for such fine people as Jenny Grossinger of Grossinger's, Arthur Winarick of the Concord and Jack Paul of Paul's.

And although I didn't get my start in the great resort area, such famous showfolk as Red Buttons, Phil Silvers, Danny Kaye,

Eddie Fisher, Jan Murray, Sid Caesar, Jerry Lewis and many, many others graduated from the Catskills to the top of the entertainment world.

If you've ever been to the Catskills, you know that a large portion of the hotel guests spend almost their entire vacations sitting on the hotel lawn talking about themselves.

And during these "sitting sessions" it is not uncommon for the guests to exaggerate a little.

Thus, on a hotel lawn, a cutter becomes a manufacturer; a teller becomes a bank president; and a hospital orderly becomes a surgeon.

I'm thinking specifically of an old friend of mine who believed he was the greatest writer of his time.

One day while he was seated on a hotel lawn he struck up a conversation with a fellow seated next to him.

"What do you do?" the fellow asked.

"I'm a writer," my friend said proudly.

"Have you written anything recently?"

"As a matter of fact, I have. I've just completed the greatest play of the century."

"Is that right? What did you call it?"

"I've entitled it *Hamlet.*"

"*Hamlet!* You must be joking. Didn't you ever hear of a fellow named Shakespeare?"

"Isn't that strange," smiled my friend, "they asked me the same question when I finished *Macbeth.*"

☺

After working like a slave for more than a year, the shy cutter approached his boss.

"I'd like to remind you, that when I came to work for you, you told me that I could expect a substantial increase within twelve months," he began.

"So I did," smiled the top man. "Well, starting next month there'll be an extra two dollars in your pay envelope—even though I think you still have a lot to learn."

"You're so right," grunted the unhappy employee, "for years I thought substantial was a ten dollar word."

☺

A top garment center salesman went to the Catskills for a well-earned vacation. However, while he was there tragedy struck. He overexerted himself on the golf course, had a heart attack, and passed away.

When his boss heard of his untimely demise, he was beside himself. Immediately, he wired the hotel:

ARRANGE BEST FUNERAL MONEY CAN BUY. BUT FIRST SEND BACK JACK'S SAMPLES!

☺

Fabrics man Nat Marcus tells of a fellow who was in such a hurry to get to the Concord to spend his annual two-week vacation that he lost control of his car just outside Monticello, and ran into a telephone pole.

When he regained his senses he found himself lying atop several phone wires.

"Thank goodness," he sighed. "It's a harp!"

☺

Murray Oliphant knew an eccentric old fellow who was going to the Catskills for his two-week vacation. Not being a member of the monied class, the old gentleman didn't own a car, so he had to travel by bus. But he was a jolly sort and this didn't bother him. Besides, this was his first trip to the Borscht Belt and he was as excited as a small boy. Even the fact that there were no seats available when he boarded the bus at Jerome Avenue in the Bronx didn't faze him. He simply planted himself in the middle of the aisle and proceeded to sing brightly: "I'm going to the Catskills; I'm going to the Catskills."

The bus driver noticed the lone standee and called out, "Move to the back of the bus, Pop."

But the gay old blade continued to sing out his ditty as the driver pulled away from the curb.

In a few minutes, the driver, visibly annoyed, turned around and snarled, "Hey, you, I told you to get to the back. Now, move!"

Unperturbed, the old gentleman repeated the musical: "I'm going to the Catskills; I'm going to the Catskills."

A couple of miles later, the bus driver was nearing the end of his patience. "Listen, you," he shouted, "either you get back there where you belong or I'm going to stop the bus and personally throw your valise out the window!"

Still there was no response from the preoccupied old codger whose tuneful chant continued uninterrupted.

The driver managed to contain himself for a mile or two more, but his temper was nearing the breaking point.

"I told you I'd throw your valise out the window," he yelled at the rear-view mirror, "and in two more minutes, Dad, that's just where it's going if you don't make tracks."

"I'm going to the Catskills; I'm going to the Catskills," sang the old man happily in reply.

The bus driver could stand no more. Fuming with rage, he slammed his foot down on the brake, pulled the bus over to the side of the road, and stormed back to where the troublesome passenger was standing. He picked up the valise and tossed it out the nearest window.

Still the old guy was undisturbed. After a brief pause, his song began anew: "I'm going to the Catskills; I'm going to the Catskills . . . I won't call up the police; I didn't bring a valise . . . I'm going to the Catskills. . . ."

Phil Greenwald, who books acts at the Concord, roared when I told him this one:

The father, who had been approached by his daughter's steady, told the young man, "I see no reason why you shouldn't marry my daughter—if you can support a family."

"I'm prepared to do that, sir."

"Good," replied the patriarch, holding out his hand. "Counting my daughter, there are seven of us."

Advertising executive Milton Blackstone tells about the two cellmates who whiled away their sentences bragging about the criminal "firsts" in their respective families.

"When they invented the pay telephone," boasted one, "my grandfather was the first guy to use a slug."

"That's nothing," scoffed the other. "My grandmother was the first woman—and there wasn't any man ahead of her either—to get ten years for petty larceny."

"Ten years! What did she steal?"

"A coat hanger at Grossinger's."

"A coat hanger! You mean to tell me your grandmother got ten years for stealing a coat hanger! She must have polished off the cop who arrested her to get that kind of a stretch."

"No-o-o," admitted the braggart, "the coat hanger happened to be attached to a mink coat."

☺

In the same prison, according to Morty Curtis of Grossinger's, there was a thief who was none too bright. It seems he had broken into a Monticello dress shop three times.

"What did you steal that took three break-ins?" asked a fellow prisoner. "Three burglaries in one place . . . crazy!"

"I was only after one dress for my wife," explained the naive thief, "and she kept making me change it."

☺

If you've ever been to the Catskills, you know that the staffs of many hotels are made up entirely of college students who are trying to save up a little money for next year's tuition. Thus, almost every season the turnover in these hotels is almost 100 per cent.

Gus Feldman, of Sanjo Dresses, likes the one about Herb Schier, an old Catskill waiter, who returned to a hotel where he had worked a few years before. He walked into the help's quarters and knocked at the door of his old room.

"Yes?" queried the occupant of the room as he opened the door.

"This was my room when I worked here," Herb explained, "do you mind if I come in and look around?"

"Oh not at all," replied the current tenant.

As he entered the room, Herb glanced around and smiled nostalgically. "Same old room, same old windows and same old furniture," he mused. Then he looked at the closet and his smile broadened. "And same old closet." He walked over and opened the door. There stood a girl, rigid with terror.

"This is my sister," explained the young waiter.

"Yes, sir," said Herb, "same old story!"

☺

There's no doubt about it. The story is the same, but the girls are different. "Every summer," says agent Al Perry, "the girls go to the Catskills to look for husbands . . . and the husbands go to look for girls."

☺

When a husband and wife go to the mountains, each takes special pains to keep an eye on the other.

A married couple was seated in the dining room of the Con-

cord. While they were eating, a shapely lass passed by.

"That's an attractive woman," commented the husband.

"You mean the one with the dyed red hair and the cheap-looking platform shoes?"

"Yes, she does have red hair."

"With her complexion she should never wear that purplish color," remarked the wife. "Her dress is badly cut through the middle and hangs unevenly in the back. She shouldn't wear such light stockings, and I hate green nail polish."

"I still say she's attractive," said the husband.

"Of course, I can't say for sure," answered the wife, "I really didn't take a good look at her!"

☺

Bert Roth and Al Rappoport of D.R.A. Dresses, once employed a terrific salesman whose name was Murray. Murray was well-liked by all the customers and continually outsold all the other salesmen. Since he always made a lot of money, he really should have been quite a happy fellow. However, he wasn't. It seems that Murray looked exactly like Mario Lanza.

At first it didn't bother him too much. Total strangers would stop him in the street and ask for his autograph. Others would slap him on the back and say, "Hi, Mario, what's new?"

And to all of them Murray would answer politely. "There's been a mistake. You've got the wrong guy. I'm not Mario Lanza."

But, try as he would, Murray continually ran up against this situation until finally it got completely out of hand. He had no privacy and he was being pestered to death.

Noticing that Murray was upset, Bert Roth suggested that he take a vacation in the Catskills and forget about the whole thing.

So Murray went to the mountains. He checked into Paul's, but before he could sign his name, the desk clerk extended his hand and said, "This sure is an honor. I've always wanted to meet you, Mr. Lanza."

Murray had had enough. "I'm not Mario Lanza!" he screamed,

and I don't want you to call me that! My name is Murray: M-U-R-R-A-Y . . . do you hear me!"

And with that he grabbed his key and stomped up to his room. He turned the key, walked in, and what do you think he saw? There, seated on a chair, was the most beautiful girl he had ever seen in his whole life.

"Oh," she sighed, "I've wanted to meet you all my life, Mario. You're wonderful! I've waited so long for this moment."

And Murray threw back his head and began to sing loudly, "BE MY LOVE!"

Mark Wachs, the witty New York gag-writer, tells about an-another Catskill romeo.

This one had just stepped into the lobby of a Catskill hotel when he spotted a gorgeous redhead. They exchanged significant looks and smiles. In a moment they were at the desk together registering as "Mr. and Mrs. Max Cohen."

The next morning Max was the picture of contentment as he checked out. But the smiles disappeared quickly when his bill was announced.

"Five hundred dollars!" he repeated incredulously. "Why, I've only been here one night!"

"I know," replied the clerk. "But your wife has been here for three months."

Every Catskill resort has a pool. Generally, that's the place where the boys and girls meet and plan for the rest of the day . . . and sometimes for the rest of their lives!

George and Abe Mitchell, of Mitchell Paper Stock, laughed when I told them this Mrs. Finster yarn.

Mrs. F. was vacationing in the Catskills. She had gone for

her health, but so it shouldn't be a total loss, she was keeping an eye peeled for a young man for Rosie, her eldest.

One afternoon she was seated by the pool when it occurred to her that the handsome young lifeguard might be a likely prospect.

"Young man," she called, "come and talk to an old lady." When he was standing by her chair, she said, "Sit down, you look like a nice young man. I'd like you to meet my daughter."

"What does she look like?" asked the youth.

"She's a wonderful girl," gushed Mrs. Finster, "and very intelligent. She graduated from Hunter with honors."

"Oh, yes? And is she good-looking?"

"And now she's got a job teaching on Long Island. She makes all her own clothes and she can cook better than her own mother."

"She sounds like a nice girl. But is she pretty?"

"Her uncle in the clothing business gave her $25,000 when she graduated, and . . ."

"Is she here with you now, Mother?"

And how about the recent conversation United Audit accountant, Sam Mandelbaum, overheard at another Catskill pool?

"Helen shouldn't go in the water alone. She almost drowned yesterday and that handsome young lifeguard had to use artificial respiration," said one.

To which the other answered: "You mean Helen had to use artificial drowning."

William Bass and Jack Feit, of Bass-Feit, were seated at the edge of the pool at the Concord when they heard a fellow scream, "Help! Save me! I'm the father of 15 children!"

The lifeguard dived into the water and shouted, "Okay, mister, I'll save you, but you sure picked a fine time to brag!"

☺

And not too far away were seated a husband and a wife. The wife suspected her husband was carrying on with one of the waitresses at the hotel.

"I'm warning you!" she bawled, "If you don't stop drinking and running after women, I'm going to throw myself into the pool and drown myself."

"Promises, promises," sneered the husband, "that's all I ever get—promises."

☺

Judy Gibbs, of Judy Formals, had a very homely girl-friend who was finding it extremely difficult to hook a man.

"Let's go up to the Concord," suggested her father. "There are a lot of eligible young men up there."

But after three days at the famous resort, the poor girl hadn't even had a nibble even though there were plenty of fish available.

Finally, the father hatched a scheme. Though Rosalie was an excellent swimmer, her father advised her to forget it for the purposes of the plan. She should wait at the pool for Papa's signal to fall in accidentally on purpose.

That afternoon they were strolling by the pool, and Papa said, "Now."

Dutifully Rosalie toppled into the water and began flailing about helplessly. In a few moments a handsome young man was pulling her to safety.

"My boy," beamed Papa, "that was a very courageous act indeed. There's too little heroism in the modern world, and I believe in rewarding a hero. I'm going to give you a check for $300, young man. And not only that—though it pains me to lose her, I'm going to give you the hand of this fragile flower you've rescued from the deep—my daughter Rosalie . . ."

"Never mind the hearts and flowers, mister," retorted the youthful hero. "But I'll take your money. It's the least you can do for pushing me in the pool."

Harry Rosen, ad boss of the New York *Post*, knows another father who took his daughter to the Catskills to get a man. He pointed out an old fellow to his daughter.

"There's a good catch," said father.

"But Dad," she complained, don't you think he's a little too old to be considered eligible?"

"My dear girl," said her father, "he's a little too eligible to be considered old."

Although most people think of the Catskills as exclusively a resort area, there are still many farms scattered throughout the area.

Joe Gordon, of Petite Lady Dresses, knew a woman whose husband had recently passed away. Since they had been a devoted couple, the wife was completely broken up by his passing.

"Why don't you go to a farm in the Catskills," a friend advised. "The fresh air and sunshine will do you good, and maybe you won't think about Seymour so much."

The wife agreed, and the next day she headed toward the Borscht Belt. Once on the farm, she was in much better spirits. She ate good wholesome food, got plenty of sleep, and for exercise she took long walks.

One afternoon while she was walking through the pasture, she heard her departed husband's voice.

"Sara," he called, "this is me, Seymour."

"Oh, my darling," she called, "how are you?"

"Well," he began, "I've come back to life. Right now, I'm standing in a pasture, not far from where you are, surrounded by 500 big healthy cows."

"Oh," moaned his wife, "it must be terrible with all those cows around."

"It's not really so bad," soothed her husband, "because you see dear, I've come back as a bull!"

☺

Paul Grossinger, of the famed resort, knew a famous world traveler who, being of the Jewish faith, always made it a point to spend Yom Kippur at Grossinger's.

For years the traveler had mapped out his schedule and always made sure that when that day rolled around he would be praying at the temple of the famed hotel.

But one year, due to a very important assignment, he was unable to make it, and when the high holy day rolled around, he found himself in China.

Truly disturbed by his inability to be at the hotel for the

holiday, the traveler walked unhappily down the streets of Nanking brooding over the turn of events.

While he was walking, he happened to look up, and was amazed to see a temple with a Jewish star in front. He walked in, and was really astonished to see a Chinese rabbi conducting the services. He walked over to the side of the room, picked up a prayer shawl, and joined in the services.

Several minutes after he was seated, the rabbi walked over to him, stared, and then asked, "Are you Jewish?"

"Well, er—yes I am," said the traveler.

The rabbi eyed him again and then said, "Well, you certainly don't look it!"

AND BEFORE WE LEAVE THE CATSKILLS

REMEMBER WHAT CONFUCIUS COHEN SAYS:

MEN BETTER START LAUGHING

AT GIRL'S BATHING SUITS

BECAUSE SOON THERE WILL BE

NOTHING TO LAUGH AT

IT'S
A PLEASURE TO
MEET THE PRESS

Of all the people I've known during the years I've been in show business, none have been as warm and receptive as the many columnists and reporters I've met and dealt with.

I remember when I was making the transition from a Garment Center gagster to a night club entertainer how these guys and gals encouraged me. Since the beginning of my career, I've always been warmly appreciative of the wonderful treatment accorded me by all the members of the Fourth Estate. As a small token of gratitude, I devote this chapter to them.

Since ladies come first, it seems only fitting that I start off with the female members of the press:

Muriel Fischer, the gal who gets all those scoops for the New York *World-Telegram*, always finds time to listen to my latest stories. At our last meeting, Muriel applauded when I told her the one about the rather obnoxious woman who was boasting to her friend about the wonderful achievements of her ancestors.

127

"My great-great-great-great grandfather fought with Washington," she said proudly.

"Is that right?"

"And my great-great-great grandfather fought with Jackson."

"Really?"

"Not only that, my great-great grandfather fought with Grant."

"No kidding."

"And my grandfather fought with Pershing and my husband fought with Eisenhower."

"Say," said her friend, "your family didn't get along with anybody, did they?"

The New York *Herald Tribune*'s Marie Torre loves the one about the fellow who was awakened by a burglar. Grabbing his shotgun, the house owner raced downstairs and confronted the crook.

"Okay, you," he threatened, "put all that stuff back in the safe."

"But I can't," protested the bandit, "half of it belongs next door!"

Pretty Atra Baer, the clever TV critic of the New York *Journal-American*, likes the one about the vain young woman who was taking her first driving lesson.

"Richard," she told her husband, "that little mirror up here isn't set right."

"Why sure it is, dear," replied her spouse.

"Oh, no, it isn't," insisted his wife. "I can't see myself in it. All I can see is the cars behind me!"

TV critic Harriet Van Horne is a wonderful girl with a terrific sense of humor. Her favorite story deals with the henpecked husband who was spending an infrequent night out with the boys. However, while the other fellows were relaxing and playing cards, the little fellow seemed tense and worried. Presently, he told them that it was getting late and that he had to go home.

"Why are you leaving so early, Bob?" one fellow asked.

"Well, er—you see, er—I don't like to leave my wife . . ."

"Why are you so afraid of her? What are you, a man or a mouse?"

"Why, I'm a man of course," the husband answered quickly.

"Really? What makes you so sure of that?"

"Because my wife is afraid of mice."

Hedda Hopper, who writes about Hollywood for the New York *Daily News* and other papers, attended a very exclusive Beverly Hills party and happened to overhear the following conversation between two catty females:

First Girl: (who is showing an expensive pearl necklace she received from an admirer to her friend) "Darling, they're genuine pearls . . . in case you've never seen the real thing before."

SECOND GIRL: "Oh, I know real pearls when I see them . . . no matter how small they are."

☺

And Louella Parsons claims that the trouble with most newly-married girls is their lack of understanding of their husbands' salaries. The way they handle the budget, usually there's too much month left over at the end of the money.

☺

The New York *Daily Mirror*'s Frances Merron tells of the Garment Center manufacturer who died and went to heaven.

When he arrived, he was greeted by St. Peter who began showing him around. The heavenly gate-keeper showed him the beautiful scenery, the wonderful facilities, and the people, who all appeared extremely happy.

After showing the newcomer the entire layout, St. Peter was hurt because the chap seemed completely unimpressed. Finally, he asked, "You mean you don't like it up here?"

"It's not that," answered the man from 38th Street, "but Miami's got better hotels."

☺

Frank Farrell of the *New York World Telegram & Sun* has a psychologist friend who told him the following story:

Two silk manufacturers requiring a private secretary called in a psychologist. After testing more than 30 applicants, the psychologist eliminated all but three of them.

In the final test, the first girl was called in: "How much is three and three?" the dome prober asked.

"Six," she replied.

The second girl was asked the same question and replied, "It could be thirty-three."

The third one answered, "It could be six and it could be thirty-three."

When the girls left the room, the psychologist turned proudly to the partners and said, "That's logic for you. You noted that the first girl gave the obvious answer, the second girl showed more imagination, and the third showed both practicality and imagination. Now which girl will you hire?"

The partners moved over to the opposite corner of the room, conferred briefly and then announced their decision, "We'll take the blonde in the sweater."

Earl Wilson, who's always telling those gay girlie gags, loves the one about the middle-aged woman who was having trouble falling asleep. She tried aspirin, sleeping pills, and every other known remedy in an attempt to rid herself of her insomnia. How-

ever, none did any good. Finally, as a last resort, she went to see a psychiatrist.

"Tell me," asked the head shrinker, "do you dream frequently?"

"Why, yes," she blushed. "I have the same dream every night."

"Really?" asked the psychiatrist with interest. "Tell me about it."

"Well, in this dream I'm always being pursued by the same handsome young man, and he always wants to make love to me."

"I see," mused the doc, inwardly pleased that he'd arrived at the crux of her problem so quickly. He reached into a drawer of his desk and took out two dozen pills, which he slipped into an envelope.

"Take two of these every night before retiring," he told her. "Then come back to see me in two weeks."

Two weeks later she returned to his office, her features less cheerful than before.

"What's wrong?" he asked. "Didn't the pills take effect?"

"Oh yes," she replied. "They worked fine. As a matter of fact, I haven't felt so rested in years." Then, after a moment's hesitation, she added coyly, "But frankly, doctor, I miss that young man!"

Leonard Lyons, Earl's colleague at the New York *Post*, was walking down Madison Avenue the other morning. During his stroll, he passed a pair of odd-looking fellows and overheard the pair discussing a cute little cocker spaniel one of them was taking for its morning walk.

"Oh, what a cute little pup," commented one.

"I got it for my wife," beamed the other.

"How'd you ever make a trade like that?"

Lee Mortimer, columnist, commentator, author and critic, tells about the two killers who were hired to assassinate a leading political figure of a foreign country who was touring the U.S. The pair checked his habits and learned that every evening before he dressed for dinner the foreign bigwig went to his hotel barber shop and took a shave. This occurred at exactly six o'clock every evening. Accordingly, the hoods decided to knock him off just before he took his shave.

That night, the pair strategically seated themselves in front of the barber shop at five-thirty and took up their vigil. At six, they put their hands on their pistols and watched the door anxiously. But the statesman didn't come.

"He'll be here any minute," one assured the other.

Six-thirty came and went, and there was still no sign of the diplomat.

The crooks were beginning to worry, "Do you think he'll show?" whispered one to the other.

To which his nervous associate answered, "Gee, I hope nothing happened to him."

☺

Ed Sullivan, TV M.C., columnist and former sportswriter, recalls the days when he used to cover all the top sporting events.

He specifically remembers the time when he was covering an important game at the Yankee Stadium.

A small boy was lost in the crowd and kept annoying all the fans by screaming, "Where's my mother? I'm lost!"

Distracted by the little boy's cries, people would give him nickels, dimes and quarters in an effort to keep him quiet until his mother returned. But as soon as he collected, he would start bawling again, "Where's my mother! I'm lost! I'm lost!"

Seeing the little fellow's plight, a kindly old gentleman approached him and said, "Stop crying, little fellow, I know where your mother is."

"So do I," whispered the kid. "But keep it quiet, will ya! Keep it quiet!"

☺

Hy Gardner of the New York *Herald Tribune,* who is also a TV celebrity, was discussing grandmothers with John Crosby, the radio-TV columnist for the same paper.

"No one is prouder than a grandmother," Hy was saying. "They have forgotten all the wet diapers and hard work associated with bringing up a baby. All they notice is how many steps their little darlings can take, the cute words of wisdom that come out of the mouths of the little angels, and how many times the sweet little things kissed grandma on her last visit."

"I know exactly what you mean, Hy," answered John. "Last week, while I was walking through the park, I met a neighbor of mine who was taking her two little grandsons for a walk. I waved to her and said, 'You have very nice looking grandchildren, Mrs. Brown. How old are they?'

"Smiling proudly, she said, 'The lawyer is four and the doctor is six.'"

☺

Bob Sylvester, who writes those comical columns for the New York *Daily News,* recently visited a friend who owns a chain of hardware stores.

The fellow lives on Riverside Drive, and when Bob walked into the house, he was very impressed by the layout and furnishings. But when he stepped into the living room, he was shocked to see the fellow's little three-year-old son holding a hammer in his hand and knocking nails into the piano, the chairs, tables, and even the floor.

"That seems like an expensive way for your son to play," he told his host.

"Oh, not at all," his friend assured him. "You see, I don't pay for the nails!"

Sid Fields, who writes the ever popular "Only Human" column for the New York *Daily Mirror* loves the one about the prominent psychiatrist who was vacationing in Las Vegas. Although the head shrinker wasn't a gambling man, he would go to the gambling casino every night in order to study the reactions of the people who were betting in the various games of chance. However, no matter where he'd begin, the psychiatrist would always wind up watching the poker players.

Noticing the doctor's fascination for the poker games, one player asked him about it.

"Well, let's put it this way," said the medical man, "I've come to the conclusion that a good poker player is the type who could hold down any kind of job."

"But doc," replied the card shark, "what would a good poker player want with a job!"

Marty Burden of the New York *Post* recently told me about a young college student who was called into his English professor's office.

"Young man," began the learned man, "who wrote that excellent essay you submitted to me yesterday?"

"I did," replied the student quickly.

"Is that so?" smiled the professor. Then, in a voice dripping with sarcasm, he added, "To think that in my lifetime I'd come face to face with Ralph Waldo Emerson!"

Nick Kenny, who writes those pearls of wisdom for the New York *Daily Mirror*, once knew a comedian who was asked to entertain at a policemen's benefit ball. Being a charitable guy, the comic agreed. On the night before the show, the Police Commissioner called the comic aside. "I'll have to audition you before you go on," the top cop told him.

"Is that so?" asked the comedian innocently. He gazed thoughtfully at the floor for a moment and then added, "I wonder if you'd mind waiting here for a minute. I won't be long."

"Where are you going?"

"Out to audition the nearest burglar alarm. I want to see how good you are!"

Lovable Louis Sobol, dean of the New York *Journal American* staff overheard the following conversation between two unhappy husbands.

"Does your wife listen to you?" asked one.

"The only time my wife shows the slightest interest in my conversation," his friend answered sadly, "is when I'm talking to another woman."

When I was breaking into show business, Lee Mortimer of the New York *Daily Mirror*, was one of my greatest boosters. I've never forgotten this, and every time we meet, we both break into big, broad smiles. Then we exchange the stories we've collected since our last meeting. Recently, I broke Lee up with the tale about the young mother who was called to school because her little Melvin's deportment was not all that it should be. It just so happened that Melvin's mother had graduated from Barnard and had majored in—you guessed it—psychology. Not only that—she had read all the latest books on the subject. When Mom arrived in school she wasn't at all what the teacher had expected.

"Your son is very noisy and disrupts my class," said the teacher severely.

"Let me warn you," began the mother quickly, "you must never raise your hand to Melvin. He is a very sensitive child and physical punishment directed against him may cause a trauma. The poor boy, I'm afraid, has paranoic tendencies. He's always suspecting people of plotting against him. So if you are convinced he needs discipline . . . hit him while he's looking."

Harold's mother—Harold was a classmate of Melvin—dealt with a similar problem a bit differently. She, too, had received reports that her boy's conduct was troublesome. But she hadn't read any psychology books.

When she came to visit the teacher, she, too, explained that her Harold was sensitive. However, she was perfectly aware that he could be a behavior problem.

The question was: how to discipline Harold without scarring his sensitive nature.

"The thing to do is scare him," she advised the teacher. "If he acts up and you just can't stand it anymore, hit the boy in front of him."

☺

Ben Gross and Sid Shalit, radio and TV critics for the New York *Daily News* recently asked a 12-year-old boy his opinion of the romantic programs as compared to the rip-roaring westerns.

"I can't stand that mushy stuff," came the expected response. "But I got a system. Whenever my mother and father watch one of those pictures with a lot of huggin' and kissin', I just pretend the guy is chokin' the dame to death."

☺

Danton Walker, one of the long-time top Broadway columnists, likes the one about the two New Yorkers who went on a hunting trip. One took a quart of liquor and the other brought a jug of coffee. Both drank heartily. Then they found the right spot and waited for their prey.

After waiting about two hours, a lone duck appeared 50 feet away. Lifting up his rifle, the coffee drinker shot, and missed. From further back, the liquor drinker shot and hit the bird right between the eyes.

"Good shooting," said the coffee man.

"It wash nothin'" answered his inebriated pal. "With a flock like that, I should have brought down 10 or 12!"

☺

Abel Green, the beloved editor of *Variety*, is one of the most popular guys in show business. Everyone agrees that Abel's got talent and wit to burn. Not too long ago, I ran into him on Broadway and he told me about the southern politican who boarded the train in Raleigh, North Carolina, and told the porter, "Ah'm to be sworn in as a membah of Congress in Washington tomorrow morning. Listen to what Ah tell you, boy. When we get to Washington, even if Ah'm *sound asleep*, you put me off this train."

Of course, the porter promised to do as the Representative-elect wished. But the next morning when the train pulled into Penn Station in New York, the politician was fast asleep in his berth. As the train jogged to a halt, he woke up and gazed, baffled, out the window. When he realized where he was, he hit the ceiling. He scrambled out of his berth and raced up the aisle, bellowing: "Where's that porter! Let me at him! Ah'll tear him limb from limb!"

Meanwhile, the porter had wisely hidden behind a seat. Another porter discovered his friend where he was crouching and asked, "What's the matter with that man running around and screaming like that? Boy, is he mad! He looking for you?"

"He's looking for me, all right," said the guilty porter, "and he sure *is* mad, but nothing compared to the man I put off in Washington."

The A.P.'s Hal Boyle likes to tell the one about the press agent who was forever pestering a certain columnist. The drum beater had a new client and wanted to get an item in the paper to impress him. Finally, after several calls, the persistent fellow got through to his man.

"I've been trying to see you for almost a month. Can I set an appointment for sometime next week?" he asked.

"Well," stalled the columnist, "why don't you get in touch with my secretary?"

And the p.a. quickly replied, "I did. So last night we had a wonderful time. But I still want to see you!"

Ted Green, of *Radio Daily*, was standing on Broadway when he witnessed the following scene. It seems that a cute little blonde was standing in front of the Paramount waiting for her beau. While she was standing there, a middle-aged wolf walked

up to her, smiled, and said, "Say, you're a doll. Where've you been all my life?"

The girl looked him up and down and said drily, "Well, for the first half of it, I wasn't even born."

☺

Clark Kinnaird, author and columnist, for King Features, while seated at his desk, overheard one copy boy tell another about the haughty career woman who was forced to travel by a devious route in order to reach Chicago where she had an important business appointment. Getting off the train late at night at the little village which was a transfer point on the railroad, she was dismayed to learn she had missed the mainliner. There wouldn't be another until morning.

Since there was nothing else to do but to spend the night in this one horse town, she asked the aged baggage master about hotels.

"Ain't got no hotel in this town," he informed her.

"Oh come now, my good man, where am I going to sleep to-night?"

"With the station master, I guess," said the old man slyly.

"How dare you!" came the indignant reply. "I'll have you know I'm a lady!"

"So's the station master, ma'am," chuckled the old man.

☺

Bob Williams, the radio and TV columnist for the New York *Post*, tells about Ed Brown, a stubborn old man, who simply refused to carry an umbrella, wear rubbers on a rainy day, or otherwise cooperate with his wife's efforts to reform him.

"You never listen to advice for your own good," she nagged.

"Darn good thing for you I don't," he snorted, "or you'd still be an old maid."

☺

Meyer Berger, who writes those wonderful pieces about New York in the *Times* once had a friend who was one of the most prominent lawyers in the country. This man had a Park Avenue office which was always packed with clients. Being so successful, he was naturally in demand as a speaker at law schools and legal gatherings.

One day, the president of the university from which he had graduated called and asked him to conduct an informal round-table discussion with the members of the current graduating class. Inasmuch as he was the idol of many of these students, he felt it was his duty to go.

When they were seated around the table, one student asked the famous attorney how he happened to choose law as his calling.

"When I was a young fellow," he told them, "all I wanted to do was dance. I wanted to become another Fred Astaire and Arthur Murray wrapped into one. Every time I'd get a spare moment,

I'd call some girl and go dancing, and when I did I would forget everything. However, my parents wouldn't allow me to forget. Every chance they got they'd pull the phone from my hand and hand me a law book. Naturally, my dancing suffered. Instead of dancing, I'd spend all my time reading law books. And that gentlemen, is the reason why I am what I am today . . ."

". . . one of the world's greatest lawyers," murmured a student enviously.

"Oh, no!" snapped the great man. "One of the world's lousiest dancers."

Leo Shull, editor and publisher of *Show Business,* once took a vacation at a dude ranch. It was a nice place and Leo enjoyed all the activities. But the incident which stands out most in his mind occurred the day before he was going to leave. While standing near the corral he suddenly saw a big rattlesnake wriggling toward him. He didn't know what to do but he'd heard somewhere that if you stand still the snake will go away. While he was standing thus, a cowboy shouted from the corral, "Hey, you! Get away from there! That's a rattler. If you go near it, it will strike."

"Good Lord!" yelped Leo, "Do these things have unions too!"

Jack Gould, TV editor of the *New York Times,* reviewed a recent program in which the owner of a luggage shop told his friend, "I guess I've seen everything now."

"What do you mean by that?" asked his friend.

"Yesterday I looked up and there standing in my store was a gigantic elephant who said to me, 'I'd like to see something new in trunks.'"

Hobe Morrison, one of the top men at *Variety*, was seated with Jack Hellman in one of the better New York night spots recently, when they, as well as all the other patrons, were shocked to see an elephant walk in. He wasn't a self-conscious elephant, either. Just as if it were an everyday occurrence, the elephant sauntered up to the bar and ordered a scotch and soda.

The proprietor, fearing the reactions of his customers, sidled up to the beast and tapped him on the shank. But the elephant ignored him. Finally, the owner said, "It's been a long time since we've seen an elephant in here."

Still the elephant ignored him and looked up at the price list. Suddenly, with a toss of his trunk, he made his way to the door. When he reached it, he trumpeted, "And it'll be a long time before you'll see another one at these prices!"

Ben Rosenberg, Amusement Editor of the New York *Post*, knew an ambitious cub reporter whose first assignment might have been his last.

"There's been a bank robbery at Bayshore, Long Island," the editor barked. "Get out there and get all the facts. And hurry."

The cub raced down to his car and headed for Long Island. After he had driven through the Midtown Tunnel he jammed his foot down on the accelerator and the speedometer shot up to 90 miles an hour. In his haste, the eager reporter drove right through a house.

Jumping out of his auto, he asked the woman of the house, "How do I get to Bayshore?"

Pointing, she said, "Straight past the kitchen table and turn right at the TV set in the study!"

Sidney Skolsky, the fellow who says, "But don't get me wrong, I love Hollywood," tells of a noted star who applied for a passport to go to Europe. When she came to the question asking whether she was married, she paused for a moment and then quickly wrote: "OCCASIONALLY."

☺

Columnist Bugs Baer, who writes those clever quips for the *Journal-American*, recently met an old friend whom he hadn't seen for several years.

"How's your wife?" Bugs asked, "has she changed much?"

"Plenty," answered his friend ruefully. "My habits, my clothes and my friends."

☺

Columnist Irving Hoffman has a friend who believes the American way of judging a movie is as follows: condemning it for being immoral; attending it to see if it's as shocking as advertised; and then kicking because the spicy parts have been cut out.

☺

Bennett Cerf, the author-columnist-humorist, knew a railroad claim agent who was teaching his wife to drive. Suddenly, the brakes failed on a steep downhill grade.

"I can't stop!" she screamed. "What shall I do?"

"Brace yourself," advised her spouse, "and try to hit something cheap."

☺

Jim O'Connor, the popular drama critic of the *Journal-American* tells of the teenager who explained why he preferred to sit in the last seat in the classroom.

"Sitting there I get last chance at a question," the youngster said. "By then it's almost impossible to guess wrong."

☺

Robert Dana, of the *World Telegram & Sun* knew a young bride who told her spouse, "Darling, I'm afraid your dinner is a little burned tonight."

"The hell you say!" exclaimed her husband. "Don't tell me they had a fire at the delicatessen!"

☺

The *Daily Mirror*'s Frank Quinn was lunching in the Pen & Pencil when he overheard the following heart-to-heart talk between a boss and his employee:

"Bill, how is it you never come to work on time anymore?"

"Well, boss, it's like this," explained Bill. "You've done such a thorough job of educating me not to be a clock-watcher during office hours that I've lost the habit of watching it at home too!"

☺

Hinson Styles, also of the New York *Daily Mirror*, always has a good story for me whenever we meet. Recently he told me about two business partners who had never had an argument in thirty years. However, one weekend one of the pair came down with the flu and missed a few days at the office.

About the third day, the partner at work phoned his ailing friend and announced, "I just found $10,000 missing from the safe. What shall I do?"

To which his ailing friend quickly replied, "Put it back!"

☺

Statistics cannot always be relied upon, reports writer Paul Denis.

For instance, he cites an item to the effect that in the United States there are only 87 women who are hunters and trappers.

☺

Mel Heimer, who writes those witty columns for King Features, has a friend whose son is a freshman at college. The boy, it seems, is deeply interested in the theater.

Recently the proud papa received a letter from his son in which the lad enthusiastically announced that he'd landed a part in a school play. "I play a man who's been married for twenty years," the boy wrote.

"Good luck, son," his old man wrote back. "Keep up the good work and before you know it they'll be giving you a speaking part."

☺

Frank Coniff, the *Journal-American* columnist, has a wonderful sense of humor. Not too long ago he told me about the football player and his girl who were standing on the sidelines watching the rest of the team scrimmage. It was obvious that a tall end was the star of the team.

"Next year," said the fellow to his girl, "Jim is going to be our best man."

"Oh darling," the girl trilled, giving him a quick kiss on the cheek, "what a nice way to ask me!"

☺

Marvin Kirsch and Joe Morris, two of the top men at *Radio Daily*, once employed a reporter who had a knack for coming up with the best stories. However, in the love department the guy batted .000. He rarely went out with girls and whenever he did get up enough nerve to ask one, the evening generally turned out to be a disaster.

This went on for many years, until finally the timid Lothario met a middle-aged spinster he liked. He dated her several times, and he was sure she shared his feelings. He decided to ask her to marry him and he stayed awake nights planning his approach. But, plot and scheme as he might, once they were together, his

courage would fail him. Finally, he decided that the only way he could untie his tongue would be by calling and asking her over the phone. Resolutely, he dialed her number.

"Is this Alma?" he demanded.

"This is Alma."

"Look here, will you marry me?"

"Why, of course," answered Alma quickly. "Who is this, please?"

Harry Hershfield, who has been making humor headlines these many years, had a conscientious bookkeeper who showed up at his office one morning looking completely worn-out.

"You must have had a big evening," said one of his associates.

"It isn't that," yawned the bookkeeper. "I couldn't get to

sleep so I started counting sheep. But I made a mistake, and it took me all night to find it."

☺

AND BEFORE WE GO TO THE NEXT CHAPTER
REMEMBER WHAT CONFUCIUS COHEN SAYS:
NEWSPAPER WHICH PRINTS PICTURE
OF GIRL WEARING FALSIES
IS GUILTY OF TOPOGRAPHICAL ERROR.

THERE'S
NO PEOPLE LIKE
SHOW PEOPLE

There's no people like show people. They're gay, they're talented and they're lovable. Even more important, they're generous.

Almost daily, one reads or hears about a forthcoming marathon at which a name star will devote his time to raising money for the unfortunate and afflicted.

Such stars as Dean Martin, Jerry Lewis, Milton Berle, Martha Raye, Eddie Cantor, Joey Adams, Danny Kaye, George Jessel, Harry Hershfield and many others have unselfishly given their time and energies to helping the sick and needy.

Walter Winchell is another; he has devoted a tremendous amount of time and energy to creating and guiding the Damon Runyon Cancer Fund.

Dean Martin, who used to team up with Jerry Lewis on those Muscular Dystrophy Marathons, acts as a double threat now that he's a single. Besides singing, Dean keeps the audience in stitches with his stories.

One of Dean's favorites deals with a hobo who walked up to the front door of a large mansion.

"Well?" asked the housekeeper, "what can I do for you?"

"Oh nothin' much, ma'am," he assured her, "I just wondered whether I could cut your grass for my dinner?"

"Of course," replied the understanding housekeeper, "but you don't have to cut it. Eat it just as it is."

☺

On a marathon, Jerry Lewis jumps, yells, mugs, mimics, and tells jokes like this one:

A husband and wife were arguing outside the Latin Quarter.

"What do you mean by coming home at 4 A.M. the other night? If I've told you once, I've told you a hundred times . . ."

"All right, dear," her spouse answered meekly, "I won't come home that early again."

☺

Milton Berle, the wonderful Mr. Television who's currently leaving them laughing at the better night spots around the country, recently told me about a very exclusive eatery in Las Vegas.

The place is so fancy that when somebody orders Russian dressing, the waiter puts on Russian clothes to serve the dish. And when a customer orders Hungarian goulash, the waiter puts on a Hungarian costume.

"But after I ate there," says Miltie sorrowfully, "the cops closed the place down. I never should have ordered that salad without dressing."

☺

Martha Raye, who owned Miami's "Five O'Clock Club" when I worked there, knew a girl who registered at a Miami employ-ment bureau.

"How would you like a job as an airline stewardess?" asked the interviewer.

"Sure," she agreed, "it will give me a chance to meet men."

"But that's silly," chided the interviewer, "you can meet men on practically any job."

"Strapped down?"

☻

Eddie Cantor likes the one about the old man who was confronted by the conductor.

"Where's your ticket?" asked the conductor.

"To tell the truth," the old codger began, "I haven't got a ticket. My daughter is getting married in New York today, and it wouldn't look good if I'm not there. Look at me. I'm an old man. What would you gain by throwing me off this train? Please, let me go to the wedding."

The conductor looked at him for a few moments and then said, "Okay buddy, I'll give you a break. But keep very quiet so that nobody notices you."

"Oh, thank you," answered the old man. He sank into his chair and the conductor moved along.

As he was walking, he suddenly spied another stowaway behind a chair. Yanking the fellow out by the collar, the conductor shouted, "What's going on here, anyway? Where's your ticket?"

The second fellow was obviously frightened. He pointed down the car to the first stowaway. "*I* don't know anything about any tickets, but he invited me to the wedding!"

☺

Joey Adams, the prosperous author, scholar and comedian, has a friend whose little boy shows considerable promise. One day after school he told his father that he'd decided he wanted to enter politics when he grew up.

"That sounds like a fine ambition," said the father. Then he told the lad that they would take a trip to Washington the following weekend and see how things were done in the capital.

First they took a tour of all the famous sights—from the Lincoln Memorial to the FBI building—and then they went to the Senate building to watch the goings-on from the gallery. As they walked in, the boy spotted a chaplain seated in a far corner of the chamber. "Daddy," said the little boy, "is the chaplain there to pray for the Senators?"

"As a matter of fact," his elder answered, "the chaplain looks at the Senators and then prays for the country!"

☺

Danny Kaye frequently entertains at the Palladium in London where he draws standing-room-only crowds. On free afternoons he loves to roam around the city or take in matinees.

On one such afternoon he took in a play that was being received with the reserve we've come to associate with the British (which has never been in evidence among Danny's audiences).

As the play was letting out, Danny overheard the play being

discussed by three British army officers who were standing stiffly to one side:

"Ghastly," said one.

"Beastly," agreed the second.

The third was even more tight-lipped. He didn't say a word.

One of the vocal ones turned to him. "And what was your opinion, Colonel?" he asked.

"Came on a pass," he explained. "Hardly cricket to speak out under the circumstances, you know. But if you gentlemen will excuse me. . . ." and with that he strode to the box office a few feet away and bought a ticket.

He was back in a moment, his ticket held gingerly between thumb and forefinger.

"A stinker, gentlemen," he said tersely.

☺

George Jessel, known as the Toastmaster General, has probably appeared at more banquets than any other American. George, who's got a story for every occasion, likes the one about the well-dressed fellow who walked into a Seventh Avenue bar, demanded a double shot of rye, downed it in one gulp, tossed a five-dollar bill on the counter, and walked out. In all that time, he didn't say a word.

The bartender picked up the bill, folded it and put it in his pocket. "Can you beat a guy like that?" he remarked to the other fellows in the bar. "He comes in here, laps up a double rye, leaves a five-dollar tip, and then beats it without paying!"

☺

Hy Gardner, who is not only a clever columnist but a great raconteur as well, likes the one about the much-married Hollywood star who ran out of women to marry. In fact, he actually married one of his former wives for the second time without

153

realizing it. But in the morning, when he came down for breakfast he recognized his mother-in-law.

☺

Harry Ritz's specialties often have a Yiddish flavor:

Irving Cohen (no relation) was sent to an insane asylum by
his relatives. When the first meal was served him in the institution, he refused to eat it and yelled hysterically:

"I'm kosher—I won't eat this food—I want kosher meals!"

In order to calm Irving, the director hired a special Yiddish
cook to serve him strictly kosher meals. Naturally, he had the
best meals in the place. However, the director kept a keen eye
on Irving.

It seems that every evening after his meal, the cracked Cohen
would pull out a big cigar and smoke it. When Friday night came
around, Irving again pulled out a big stogie and began puffing
it.

The director confronted him. "Listen, Cohen, you can't expect to get away with that kind of stuff. You came here and
demanded kosher food because you said you were religious. We
went to the expense of getting you a special Yiddish cook. And
now on Friday night, when it's against your religion, you smoke
a cigar. What's the big idea?"

"Listen," countered Irving, "what's the use of arguing with me? I'm crazy, ain't I?"

☻

Morey Amsterdam likes the one about the rich old uncle who was attempting to induce his young nephew to come into his dress business with him. "But don't think you're coming in here and starting at the top," his uncle told him. "You'll begin as a partner, just like all the rest of us did."

☻

Harry Hershfield often tells the one about the grouchy wife who spent twice as much as her husband earned. She also constantly nagged the poor fellow and continually compared him with all their friends.

"Ben has a new car and Phil just bought Mary a new mink," she complained. Another one of her pet gripes was the apartment they rented. "All our friends live ten times better than we do," she whined. "They'll all laugh at us if we don't move into a more expensive neighborhood."

One night her long-suffering mate came home and told her, "Well, we won't have to move to live luxuriously. The landlord just doubled our rent."

☻

Henny Youngman tells of the well-known actress who was crazy about Swiss cheese. She had it for breakfast, lunch and supper and often in between meals. An interviewer, who had heard about her strange eating habits, decided to have some fun with her.

"Tell me," he asked her, "why do you like Swiss cheese?"

To which question the charming star quipped, "I'll tell you

if you can tell me why they put holes in Swiss cheese when it is limburger that needs the ventilation."

☺

Groucho Marx knew a slightly simple-minded foreigner who immediately headed for Reno when he got off the boat in New York. According to Groucho, the fellow said he'd heard that Reno was the place where women were made free.

☺

Barry Gray, writer, columnist, broadcaster and humanitarian, often comes up with some of the funniest I've ever heard. Typical of Barry's humor:

At a huge gathering, a female psychology student was rebuked when she stated that men were much vainer than women. Naturally, she was immediately challenged by a fellow standing near her. In order to prove her statement, she said in a clear voice that carried through the room, "It's a shame that most intelligent and sensitive men attach so little importance to the way they dress. Why, right this minute, the most cultivated man in this room is wearing the most clumsily knotted tie."

Whereupon, as if on cue, every man in the room immediately put his hand to his tie.

☺

My boy Danny Thomas always gets the audience in the mood with ones like this:

MOTHER: "Don't worry, dear. Mother will tell you everything you should know before you get married."

DAUGHTER: "That's wonderful! Then I'll be able to get as much alimony as you did."

☺

Bob Hope tells of the elderly spinster who passed a red light and paid no heed to the loud blasts from the traffic cop's whistle. He finally caught her attention and she pulled over to the side.

"Didn't you hear me whistle?" he demanded.

"Certainly I did," she answered, "but I never flirt when I'm driving."

☺

Buddy Hackett always seems to be hungry. Consequently, many of his stories deal with food.

One of his favorites is about the playboy who purchased a farm in Iowa.

"What are you going to plant?" asked a friend at his farewell party.

"Razor blades and cabbages," he answered, without blinking an eye.

"Razor blades and cabbages!" echoed the stunned guest. "What do you expect to get out of that?"

"Cole slaw."

☺

And Jack E. Leonard is another who loves to tell stories about food.

Jack often tells the one about the little old man whose doctor put him on a diet of fresh vegetables. The fellow, a bachelor, would eat his meals at a small restaurant right off Seventh Avenue. Every day he would sit at the same table and order a vegetable plate with whole wheat bread. But every day, the waitress would bring him white bread with his meal. This went on for three weeks, until one day the fellow decided he'd outwit the waitress.

"Bring me a plate of mixed vegetables with white bread," he told her.

Instead of going to the kitchen and placing the order, the girl just stood there staring at him.

"What's the matter?" he asked. "Is there something wrong?"

"Oh no, sir," answered the puzzled girl, "but aren't you the fellow who always orders whole wheat?"

Steve Allen, who is a philosopher as well as a comedian and author, contends that the best way to give advice to your children is to find out what they want and then tell them to do it.

And Jimmy Durante likes the one about the boss who walked into his office one day and asked his assistant, "Is my daughter here?"

"Yes sir," came the reply, "I saw the salesman try to kiss her."

"Did he succeed?" asked the boss.

"Oh, no, sir. She slapped his face."

"Then that wasn't my daughter!"

Jokester Jan Murray knew a prosperous garment manufacturer who fell in love with a night club singer and hired a private detective to check up on her. Two weeks later, he received the following note: "The girl in question has a good reputation. She comes from an excellent family, has many friends of high social standing, and was spoken of most highly until a few weeks ago. At that time she began running around with a garment manufacturer of questionable character."

☺

Rowdy Red Skelton's repertoire includes the impersonation of several different characters—ranging from a punch drunk fighter to a hill-billy farmer.

When Red's a punchy pugilist he prefers this one:

DRIVER: "You walk as if you owned the street!"

RED: "Yeah—and you drive as if you owned the sidewalk!"

☺

And when he's portraying a half-witted hill-billy, Red's apt to tell this one:

The minister reproved the husband for spending so much time tinkering with his new car.

"If I were you," asserted the clergyman, "I'd put my wife before my car."

"I'd sure like to," he sighed, "but I'm afraid someone might catch me at it."

☺

Jack Benny, of course, likes to tell jokes dealing with money. He fractured an audience with this one:

A prosperous silk manufacturer took an out-of-town client to his home for dinner. When the meal was over, the host took his business associate into the study and they began talking about various topics. While they were talking, the manufacturer's three young sons came running into the room. They ran around and around and made a fearful racket.

"Be good," warned the mother from the kitchen, "or you won't have any ice cream for lunch."

But the boys took no heed of their mother's warning.

"My system is better," the father told his associate. "I give Tom, my oldest son—he's seven—a dollar, and he keeps still." He handed the boy the bill, and sure enough he shut up. "And," continued the father, "I give Bob—he's five—a half-dollar and he quiets down."

"Sounds interesting," said the guest, "but what about your youngest son?"

"Oh, him," came the mother's voice from the kitchen, "he's like his father—good for nothing!"

Jackie Gleason wows any audience when he tells the one about the small-time entertainer applying for a job in a night club. "I'm the greatest entertainer in the world!" he told the owner.

"Well, what do you do?" asked the boss.

"I imitate all the big stars. I'm a mimic." Then, the fellow went into his act, impersonating everyone from James Cagney to Lassie.

Impressed, the bistro boss said, "Okay, you start on Monday night at $200 a week."

When the week was over, the boss handed the mimic a check for $50.

Amazed, the fellow went over to the owner and said, "But you promised me $200. How come I only got $50?"

"You're a mimic."

"Yes, but . . ."
"All right, then. So make like Rockefeller!"

☺

Sid Caesar's favorite goes like this:
Two old friends met in front of the Paramount Theatre on Broadway. It was a cold, wintry day with the temperature three below zero. One of the pair wore a heavy winter coat, a thick woolen muffler and a warm hat. The other had on a light top coat and wore neither hat nor scarf.

"Sam," asked his friend, "how come you go around dressed like that in weather like this? What do you want to do, catch pneumonia?"

" Oh no," assured Sam, "it's not that at all. It's just that I don't feel cold."

"You don't feel cold!"

"No, let me explain it to you. I just bought my wife a new mink coat, and when I think of how much it costs . . . I start perspiring."

☺

Red Buttons, who recently made a name for himself in Holly-wood, has been telling a lot of film funnies lately. For instance:

Walking out of a theatre after the movie debut of a famous actor's son, a critic summed up his opinion tersely with: "Just a slice off the old ham."

☺

Lucille Ball and Desi Arnaz favor this one:
In Washington, a guide was asked by a tourist about the top man's preference in food and drink.

"The President's tastes are quite simple," explained the guide. "He is easily pleased with the best of everything."

☺

Phil Silvers loves to start off with the one about the small dress shop owner who was bemoaning his fate to a friend who was visiting him.

"Oh, Benny," he complained, "at this rate I'll be out of business in no time."

"Is it that bad?"

"Just to give you an example," he began, "yesterday I sold only one dress, and today business is even worse."

"Worse? How could it be worse?"

"The woman who bought that dress yesterday, . . . well, she returned it today!"

☺

Recently I heard comedian Phil Foster delight an audience with the one about the housewife who went into a drug store and told the clerk, "Give me two packs of invisible hairpins."

"Yes, Ma'am," answered the fellow behind the counter, and began to wrap up a package for her.

"Tell me," asked the woman as he was wrapping them, "are you sure they're invisible?"

"I'll say they are," came the prompt reply. "I sold $8 worth this morning and we've been out of them for two weeks!"

☺

Joe E. Lewis, the carefree comic, loves the one about the death of a stingy, penny-pinching boss. Despite his parsimonious habits, his partner and other associates decided to give him a big funeral. On the day of the burial, the deceased was taking his final ride in a big black Cadillac. Directly behind him in the next car was his partner of 30 years.

Just before they reached the cemetery, a big coal truck pulled out from a side road into an opening between the two cars and joined the procession.

Upon seeing the coal truck in front of him, the partner commented sadly, "I knew where Harry was going, but I didn't know he had to furnish his own coal!"

The last comedian just loves to play at benefits. And the reason why I call him the last comedian is that he's the last one anybody invites. The guy I'm talking about is my brother, Phil Cohen, who is currently the leading comedian in the Garment Center. Whenever Phil appears at a benefit he tells the best jokes because he steals them from one of the best comedians in the business . . . me.

Phil's favorite deals with the Garment Center manufacturer who, after many years of scrimping and saving, had a fabulous season. Being the thrifty sort, the fellow invested his money in government bonds. When the bonds matured, he took out all the money and bought a beautiful mansion in Southampton, a very exclusive section of Long Island.

Soon after the happy man and his wife moved into their new house, they began to mingle with the other residents of the town. They were invited to everyone's home, and in turn they, too, invited their neighbors over for a pleasant social evening.

After dinner, everybody went into the drawing room. In no time at all, the guests were engrossed in a conversation about the great names in music and their wonderful contributions. Such names as Beethoven, Brahms, Bach, Tschaikowsky and Mozart were mentioned. And when Mozart's name was mentioned, the hostess commented loudly so all her guests might hear, "Mozart!

I know him well. In fact, I saw him on the red bus going to the beach this morning."

At this there was a sudden hush. All the guests looked up and stared at her. However, they were all too discreet to say anything.

Late that night, when all his guests were gone, the host confronted his wife: "You had to be such a smart aleck! You had to show off your brains! Do you know you made a fool out of yourself tonight? You ought to know that the red bus doesn't go to the beach!"

AND BEFORE WE GO TO THE NEXT CHAPTER
REMEMBER WHAT CONFUCIUS COHEN SAYS:
HE WHO GO INTO SHOW BUSINESS
OFTEN HAVE TO LIVE
FROM HAM TO MOUTH.

GAGS FOR GOURMETS

Entertaining at one of the New York niteries is fun because it gives me an opportunity to drop into some of my favorite eating places and see some of my favorite people.

These genial restaurateurs can serve up feasts of mirth as well as delectable dishes.

All who know Toots Shor feel that he is one of the greatest guys on Broadway. He's always ready to give a helping hand to a struggling performer or athlete. And his sense of humor never fails him.

His favorite joke deals with the hotel guest who was a real pain in the neck. While this fellow was at the hotel, none of the help had a moment's rest. No matter what he got, he wasn't satisfied. Needless to say, when it came time for him to check out, no one was sorry. However, the entire staff was concerned about the size of the tips this fellow would leave.

One bellhop, who didn't like to leave anything to chance, decided to give the guest a tactful reminder about tipping.

"You won't forget me, sir, will you?" he asked.

"Of course not," smiled the guest. "I'll write you every day."

☺

Danny Stradella, the lovable host of Danny's Hide-A-Way, is another fellow I'd like to see more often. Danny's favorite is about a crude fellow's first visit to a fancy restaurant. His worst habit was tucking his napkin under his chin. Naturally, this

caused the entire staff to stare at him. The *maître de* quickly ran over to the waiter who was serving the fellow and said, "Inform that man that he shouldn't wear a bib in here. But remember, do it very tactfully."

With this, the waiter walked over to the fellow and asked, "Would you like a shave and a haircut also?"

☺

Once, when I was in Danny's Hide-A-Way, I met Danny Davis. Danny's a glib guy who just loves to tell funny stories on or off stage.

One of his favorites deals with the scion of one of our wealthiest families who was a petty officer on a submarine during the last war.

"Torpedoes are expensive," the captain warned the crew. "Before you release one, make sure you're going to hit the target."

Shortly after this lecture, the million-dollar officer spotted a destroyer coming toward the sub. "Destroyer spotted on the portside," he yelled into the megaphone.

There was no answer.

"Destroyer 400 yards away!" he bellowed.

Pause.

"Two hundred yards away!" shouted the rich boy.

Still no answer, and no action.

"One hundred yards away!"

No answer; no action.

"Fifty yards away!"

Nothing.

"Fire!" bawled the playboy. "I'll pay for it!"

☺

The last time I visited his fine eatery, George Mitchell, of the Assembly Restaurant, was talking to C.B.S. producer Marlo Lewis. Both boys were in great spirits, and when they saw me the jokes began to fly.

"Did you hear the one about the manufacturer's wife who told her friend, 'I had such a wonderful time with my husband . . . he thought I was his secretary?' " asked George.

"No," I answered, "but I heard the one about the manufacturer who said there would be a lot of changes in women's styles . . . but none in men's pockets!"

☺

Then Marlo told the one about the wool cutters' convention at which Bob Hope was scheduled to appear as guest star.

When Bob walked into the place, everyone ran over to him and shook his hand. Everyone, that is, except one fellow.

"That's Bob Hope over there," his friend told him. "Don't you want to meet him?"

"Why should I want to meet him? Who's Bob Hope?" he asked.

"You never heard of Bob Hope who's in radio and television?" his friend asked in total disbelief.

"No. What's he in? Wholesale or retail?"

☺

At the Spindletop that night, I saw Alfred Bloomingdale, president of the Diners' Club, and his two associates, Ralph E. Schneider and Matty Simmons. I joined the group long enough to exchange a few funnies. For instance, there was the one about the young lover who was shopping for a gift for his latest flame. He tried an exclusive Fifth Avenue shop and pointed to a bottle of Arpège in the case. "How much?" he asked.

"Fifty dollars, sir," she smiled.

The customer emitted a long, incredulous whistle and gestured toward another bottle on the counter. "And how much is that?" he asked the saleslady.

"That," she replied crisply, "will cost you two whistles."

☺

Whenever I dine in Lindy's, I always exchange stories with the wonderful staff. Managers Ben Epton and Christopher Rudd once told me about two back country boys who walked into a very exclusive restaurant and ordered spare ribs.

After they had finished their meal, the waiter brought finger bowls and placed them before the two diners.

"I never seen glasses like that before," Clem told his friend.

"I guess we're supposed to drink from them."

"Maybe we oughta ask the waiter what they're for?"

With this they called over the man in the white jacket and asked him about the finger bowls.

"They're finger bowls," he told them. "You use them to clean your hands."

The two country boys looked at each other, and when the waiter walked away, Clem whispered to his buddy, "You see, Zeke, when you ask a silly question, you get a silly answer!"

☺

Lindy's waiters also are known for their wit. On many occasions, I've heard Sam Jaeger, Irving Weintraub, Frank Pepitone and Mickey Marks come up with real gems.

Sam once told me about a fellow who, upon leaving a restaurant, asked a waiter who hadn't served him, "Is it raining outside?"

"How would I know," sniffed the waiter, "that's not my table!"

☺

Captains of Lindy's waiters are Dave Bass, Louis Barin, Wesher Berger, and Chris Cassapoglou. These guys all believe in mind over platter and always come up with culinary chuckles.

Chris tells about the Jewish couple who dined out one evening in the neighborhood kosher delicatessen. They were amazed when a Chinese waiter approached them to take their order. But their surprise turned to shock when the suave Oriental addressed them in perfect Yiddish.

As soon as he had gone into the kitchen they motioned to the proprietor. "A Chinese waiter in a Jewish delicatessen!" exclaimed the man. "And not only that, but he talks Yiddish. How come?"

The proprietor looked around quickly and put his finger to

his lips. "Shhhh," he whispered, "he thinks I'm teaching him English!"

☺

Lindy's cashiers, Irving Areloff, Charles Dewland and Philip Davis like this one:

The two men had just dined together. Outside the restaurant, one turned to the other. "Jack," he said, "how come you left the hatcheck girl a two-dollar tip?"

"Listen," explained his friend, "isn't this new coat she gave me worth two dollars!"

(When hatcheck girl, Billy DeAngeles heard this story, she swore she wasn't the girl.)

☺

Once while lunching in Lindy's, I met Paul Waldman, the advertising genius, who told me about a psychiatrist who was so modern that he got rid of his old-fashioned couch and got a Castro convertible.

One day, a complete stranger walked into his office, opened up the Castro, and went to sleep.

Slightly annoyed, the doc woke the fellow up and asked him what he was up to.

"It's cold outside and I have nowhere to sleep," the man explained, "so I thought I'd come in here and take a quick nap."

"Oh," said the doc. "Well, the least you could do is say goodnight."

☺

Once while I was entertaining at the Latin Quarter, I invited the wonderful Tisch family to catch my act. Mr. and Mrs. Al Tisch were present as were Bob and Larry Tisch. Two of their better known hotels are the Traymore in Atlantic City and the Americana in Florida. E. M. Loewe, the popular Latin Quarter host, was seated at their table.

They all enjoyed the one about the woman who walked into a millinery store and instructed the salesgirl: "That lavender felt hat with the black plume and thick band—would you take it out of the window for me, please?"

"Of course, Ma'am," agreed the clerk, "I'd be glad to."

"Thanks so much," smiled the woman as she walked toward the exit. "That horror was giving me a turn every time I passed by."

☺

While dining recently at the Old Homestead, I bumped into Al Albert of Albert Decorators on the Grand Concourse. Al decorated my home for me.

As soon as he saw me, he asked, "Myron, did you hear about the fellow who was so rich that he served mixed greens for lunch . . . shredded fives and tens?"

"No," I retorted, "but I heard about the native who loved his fellow men . . . medium-rare."

☺

Also, at the Steak Pit that night was Mr. Yasky of the Hotel Fourteen, which is located across the street from the Copa.

He liked the one about the man who complained to the owner of a super market about the behavior of a certain clerk.

"I'll talk to him," the manager assured the customer. "After all, we aim to please."

To which the piqued customer replied, "Then why don't you close up for a day and get in some target practice?"

☺

Before dining one night, I stopped off at Victor's barber shop at 1400 Broadway. After giving me a quick haircut and shave, he remarked, "There's one thing you can say for baldness—it's neat!"

☺

My two other favorite barbers are Angelo and Eddie of the Dawn Patrol Barber Shop. Like all barbers, both boys are always full of stories. However, the last time I was there I pulled a switch and told them this one:

A retired millionaire was talking to his lazy son. "You lazy bum! Why don't you go out and find a job? When I was your age, I was working for five dollars a week in a store, and at the end of the year, I owned the place."

"Yeah?" tossed off the young one, "you wouldn't get away with that today . . . they have cash registers."

☺

I was dining in Shine's one evening with Ralph Snider and Al Taxier of Boston's Bradford Hotel, when Nat Berkowitz, of Bienen-Davis, the handbag firm, walked in. As soon as he spotted me, he came dashing over and the jokes began to fly.

First he told the one about the couple who had been married for more than 30 years and had never stopped battling. Finally, they could stand no more. She sued him for divorce and they went before the judge.

They both told their stories, and when they had finished the judge spoke: "Madam, I have decided to find for you. I'm giving you fifty dollars a week."

Hearing this, the husband spoke up: "That's handsome of you, judge—I think I'll throw in a few dollars myself."

And I came back with the one about the wife who went in front of a judge and said, "All I'm asking is that my husband should leave me the way he found me."

Slightly taken aback, the judge said, "But lady, that's impossible."

"Why impossible?" she persisted. "He found me a widow, didn't he?"

My tenpercental manager, Henri Giné of Artists Corp. of America, agent Nat Dunn, and two of my other associates, Myron H. Cohen, the Equitable Life agent, and agent Charles Rapp, were dining with me at Gross's Dairy Restaurant on Broadway and 37th Street. We were all in high spirits that evening and I began the festivities with the story about the strict, old-fashioned boss who was becoming irritated with his untidy secretary. One morning he called her into his office after noting how sloppy her desk was. He had noticed all the old slips and memos piled high upon her desk and decided to give her a pointer or two on cleanliness.

"Miss Jones," he asked, "what do you do with the slips you are through with?"

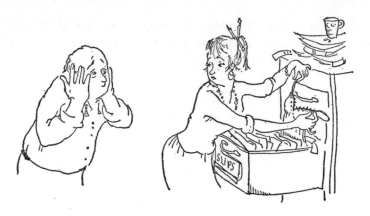

"Usually," said Miss Jones, "I give them to the Salvation Army."

☺

Then Nat countered with the tale of the handsome personnel director who, one Friday afternoon, went over to the desk of a pretty young secretary and asked, "Miss Brown, are you doing anything Sunday night?"

"Well, no," answered the girl, blushing.

"Then I suggest you get a good night's sleep and try to get to the office on time Monday morning."

☺

Seymour Klein, of the Gem Garage on 54th Street, was standing on Seventh Avenue talking to Nick Giovanna, of Chrysler-Manhattan cars. When I walked over to say hello, I noticed that Nick looked particularly unhappy.

"How's business, Nick?" I asked.

"To tell you the truth, Myron, it could be better."

"How come?" I asked.

"It's those small foreign cars. They've really made an impression," he explained. "New York is so full of them that, whenever you cross the street, you have to look left, right and down!"

AND BEFORE WE LEAVE THIS CHAPTER
REMEMBER WHAT CONFUCIUS COHEN SAYS:
PEOPLE WHO EAT LOTS OF SWEETS
WILL SOON DEVELOP LARGER SEATS.

COHEN AT HOME

I am what is called a gentleman farmer. If you're not quite sure what that is, let me explain it to you. A gentleman farmer is a fellow, who, when walking through his garden, tips his hat to all the tomatoes.

I wasn't always a farmer. Before I had my home in New City, New York, I lived on Davidson Avenue in the Bronx. *I loved the Bronx!* When I lived there, I used to go to work in the morning and come home at night and relax. But a farmer can never relax!

I go to sleep with the chickens, get up with the roosters, work like a horse, eat like a pig, and get treated like a dog.

Let me tell you something else—the fellow who said, "A farm is where you can make a living from dirt," must have been out of his mind! Believe me, I've tried!

When I first bought the place, I didn't know a thing about farming. I read all the latest books on modern methods of planting, milking and taking care of a home. Still, I felt I didn't know enough, so I decided to seek the advice of a few of my neighbors, all of whom seemed to be prosperous and to know what they were doing.

The fellow next door seemed to be especially rich. When he started showing me around his place I was amazed at the revolutionary methods he used. This fellow even tried crossing tomatoes with scotch . . . he wanted stewed tomatoes!

"I once had a hen," he told me, "that was really great. She won dozens of awards. When I put a red quilt in front of her, she would lay red eggs, when I put a green quilt before her—green eggs. A blue quilt—blue eggs. But one day someone accidentally put a plaid quilt in front of her . . . and the poor bird died trying to deliver the goods!"

Then he showed me the cows in his barn. "See that one over there," he said pointing to a healthy looking specimen. "She's a real character. I used to milk her at five o'clock every morning for more'n a year. But the morning that daylight saving time began, I got up to milk her at four o'clock. It must have given her quite a turn when I walked in at that time because when she saw me, she gave a sigh of relief and said, 'Thank God, it's you. I thought I was being robbed.' "

Seriously, though, I love my home in the country. Bill Robbins, my friend and adviser, thought it was a wonderful idea; a place for me to spend my idle hours relaxing.

About a week after I moved in, Bill pulled up in front with a small trailer attached to his car. "I brought you a little housewarming present," he smiled.

When I looked in the trailer, I was shocked to see a great big cow.

"But Bill," I protested.

"Isn't she beautiful?" he sighed. "She's a real Holstein. But to make her feel more at home, maybe we'd better change her name to Goldstein."

Jeanne Sager, my very imaginative press agent, warned, "Remember, Myron, it takes a lot of hard work before a house is completely decorated and furnished."

"That's right," added her husband, Jerry, who is a top public relations man. "A house is not a home."

☺

And Eleanor Malisoff, my pretty and very efficient secretary kidded, "Now you don't need any more writers—you can get all the spice from your garden!" But if I become a silk salesman again, will I be able to get that kind of material from my garden? Of course, I can always raise silk worms!

☺

I will always be grateful to Eddie Davis, of the famed "Leon and Eddie's," who did so much in furthering my career. Whenever Eddie, who is now in retirement in Florida, comes to the big town I always invite him to my home. The last time he came, Eddie told some of the funniest stories I've ever heard.

"Myron," he asked, "did you hear the one about the fellow who went to an art museum. . . ?"

It seems that in one room there were three statues in a row. One was posed with his arms folded and the second was pointing his finger in the direction of the third, whose arms were outstretched.

The tourist wondered if there was any connection between the statues and asked the guide for an explanation.

"Well, I'll tell you, mister," said the guide. "So many people asked me that question that I've had cards printed up explaining it."

He handed the fellow one of the cards. This was the dialogue printed there:

First Statue: Who threw that cigar butt on the floor?

Second Statue: He did!
Third Statue: Who, me?

☺

My New City neighbors—the Norbitzes to the east, and the Jukes to the west—have done a wonderful job of helping me adjust to the life of a country squire. Whenever they drop over, I always try to get a laugh out of them. The last time they visited, I used this one:

A timid office boy walked into his employer's office and announced, "I think you're wanted on the phone."

"You think!" barked the boss. "Don't you know?"

"Well sir," replied the boy, "the voice on the other end said, 'Hello, is that you, you old goat?' "

☺

My two nephews, Burton and Mitchell Cohen, always greet me with gags whenever we meet.

Burton's favorite is about the two cocker spaniels who met on the street.

One said: "Have I got problems! I think I'm headed for a nervous breakdown."

"Why don't you see a psychiatrist?" his pal suggested.

"I can't," mourned the spaniel, "I'm not allowed on the couch."

☺

And Mitchell says, "With the price of meat what it is, lamb chops should come with two pair of pants."

☺

Recently I had the honor of entertaining Judge Jonah Goldstein, who, among other things, is a life member of the Grand Street Boys' Club. That evening, Morris Landsburg, owner of Florida's Sans Souci; Herb Fine, of Goldman's, in Pleasantdale, New Jersey, and Happy Waters, of Green's, which is also in Pleasantdale; were also my guests.

The best story told that night dealt with a new employee of a dress house, who was stopped by his boss as he entered the office.

"You're twenty minutes late again!" barked the head man. "Don't you know what time we start work in this office?"

"Well, er—no, sir," stammered the new man. "They're always working when I get here."

☺

On another occasion, I entertained several of my out-of-town friends. Included in that group were: Jay Isaacson, of the Toledo Tire Company, Toledo, Ohio; Max Ackerman, an insurance man from Springfield, Massachusetts; Harry Drake, the Boston agent; and Allan Bregman, the TV and radio man from "Soupy Sales" in Detroit.

Harry Drake's story about the two wise guys who visited a nudist colony broke everyone up.

While canvassing the grounds, one of the pair, upon seeing an extremely beautiful and shapely nude stroll by, commented to his pal:

"Some doll, eh Bob? Boy, wouldn't you like to see *that* in a bathing suit!"

☺

A frequent guest at my home is Dr. Alex Rosen, the noted dentist who is responsible for the care and capping of dozens of celebrities' teeth. Alex is a great one for daffynitions. For instance, he claims that a pessimist is a guy who stops himself as he's reaching down to pick a four-leaf clover for fear he'll be bitten by a snake.

☺

Milton and Carl Shapiro and Moni Avedon of Kay Windsor dropped by one night. We got to talking and swapping stories and I told them this one:

The young fellow had just been brought before the desk sergeant for questioning.

"Have you ever been arrested before?" asked the presiding officer.

"Oh, no, sir," answered the culprit. "And I must say there's been some misunderstanding here. Oh, I know I shouldn't have done it. But pilfering my little brother's bank hardly deserves the attention of the police."

"Pilfering your little brother's bank!" repeated the desk sergeant. "What is this anyway!" And he was about to dismiss the prisoner and chew out the arresting officer when said cop intervened.

"Just a minute, just a minute," interrupted the flatfoot. "The prisoner neglected to mention that his brother happens to be a teller in the First National Bank on Pine and 20th Street."

☺

One afternoon, Kate Smith and Ted Collins, who had been busily preparing for an upcoming radio show, dropped by for a little chatter and relaxation.

No sooner had he sat down, than Ted sprung this one on me:
The rich old man, who knew that his time was running out,

had a new will drawn up. It provided that his wife would receive $5,000 a year if she remained single—and $25,000 a year if she remarried.

"That's a strange twist," said his lawyer, "how come?"

"If he marries my wife, whoever he is," said the old man. "he'll need the money—and he'll deserve it."

☺

And Kate countered with the one about the small businessman in upstate New York who after six months of valiantly trying to make ends meet decided to call it quits. He posted the following sign in his window:

OPENED BY MISTAKE.

☺

One of the reasons that I'm so fond of my New City home is that it's so convenient. Besides being so close to New York, it's also a stone's throw from Philadelphia.

Harvey and Tillie Lockman from Philadelphia's Harvey House often drop by to spend the day. Sometimes we lounge around the house and tell stories and often we have a bite to eat at Jerry Carnegie's in New City.

Jerry is a wonderful host and knows even more about food than Jack E. Leonard. The last time we were there, he tried this one on us:

The president of a prosperous Philadelphia bank was making a speech at a banquet in his honor.

"Friends," he began, "when I came to this town fifty years ago, I was a complete unknown. All I had were the clothes on my back, and a yellow handkerchief in my pocket. The balance of my worldly possessions were wrapped up in that handkerchief.

"Today I am the president of a bank. I own three department

182

stores, a filling station, four movie houses, and a beautiful home."

When he sat down his friends gathered around him and patted him on the back. One of them asked, "Ben, what did you have in that yellow handkerchief?"

"Well," smiled the oldster, "as I remember it, I had three hundred thousand dollars in cash and one hundred thousand in bonds!"

☺

Ed Mitchell, of Mitchell's Restaurant in Philly, is another who frequently drives up from the city of brotherly love. On his last visit I took him to New City's Dellwood Country Club where we had a fabulous time with host Bernie Nemeroff. As soon as we walked in the door, Bernie spotted us and came over. He asked us if we'd heard about the advertising executive who suffered such a severe shock that his hair turned charcoal gray.

"That's nothing compared to the woman who didn't want to read the 'Kinsey Report' because she was waiting for the picture to come out," countered Ed.

I added, "And what about the psychiatrist who told his wrestler patient, 'Get a grip on yourself!' "

☺

Philly real estate man, Richard I. Rubin and his son Ronnie, get a kick out of this one:

The tycoon found the attitude of his youthful associate not all that it might be. The junior lacked ambition and get-up-and-go according to the boss.

"You've got to get in there and pitch all the time," remonstrated the seasoned big shot. "Why, when I was your age I had already inherited my second million!"

☺

And Frankie Bradley, of Bradley's in the same city, claims a wedding ring is like a tourniquet—it stops the circulation.

☺

Ending a book of gags like this one is not an easy thing to do. I could go on and on until I'd find myself with an encyclopedia, but still there'd be the problem of ending it—both because the yarns just keep right on spinning themselves, and because it's hard to decide which to end with. I suppose one should sign off with The Favorite, but every day I've got a new one. That's the reason I hit on the idea of wrapping up this volume with the chapter, "Cohen At Home."

You know, when I moved out to my rural shack, I must admit I was afraid I might be lonesome. During those first few days of getting settled I felt awfully far from Manhattan. I *was* lonesome. But I hadn't reckoned on that old tradition, the housewarming.

My wife and I were unpacking boxes late one night when there came a knock at the door.

"Whoever could it be?" wondered my wife.

"It must be a salesman," I told her. "Who else would have the gall to come calling this hour of the night?"

Before I could answer the door, it flew open and there was a salesman on the threshold, all right. Not one, but dozens. Salesmen of laughs, that is—my buddies from the Friars Club.

Led by Carl Timin, they piled in like a football team in a scrimmage. When fat Jack Leonard and Jackie Gleason barreled through the door, I found myself with a sunken living room. I never did measure how far it sank, but I remember through the blur noticing a couple of miners raiding the icebox.

The neighborhood and house were still strange, and the sudden, unexpected gathering of the clan was too much for me. I kept thinking it was an all-star benefit show and got to worrying

184

about being onstage without having rehearsed my act. And I couldn't retreat into the wings, because they hadn't been built yet. You would have thought it was a benefit, too—though, like me, you might have wondered for whom—if you could have seen the all-star cast. In one corner alone there were Georgie Jessel, Milton Berle, Jack Carter, Ted Lewis, Alan King, Gene Baylos, Jackie Gleason, Sammy Davis Jr., Dick Shawn, and Lou Holtz—

each competing for the floor to share their latest funnies. As I passed this group on my way to another, I dropped a plate of cold cuts on Jackie Gleason's lap. No harm done, though. In five minutes even the spots were gone. Jackie wasn't on a diet then.

I managed to sandwich in a gag here, too. It went like this:

The aging movie producer had just divorced his fifth wife and was determined to stay out of trouble for a while when he met a movie starlet who had what it took. I don't mean she was a great actress—she had what it took to make a sixty-year-old Lothario feel like a young colt instead of a jackass.

Anyway, the producer found he was too old to change his habits, so he proposed to the young girl.

Now, there are obvious advantages in combining career and marriage when the guy happens to be a producer, and our girl wasn't blind to them. But this guy was rumored to be impossible to live with. "I hardly know what to say," hesitated the girl. "I've heard so many stories about you, and if any of them are true, I—"

"Don't listen to that gossip," interrupted the producer. "Nothing but old wives' tales."

☺

"That reminds me," ad libbed Jackie, "of the madam who squelched the gossip about her reportedly coming from a former 'girl' of hers with, 'You wouldn't listen to that old roomer!'"

☺

Between a helpless chuckle and a groan, I moved to another corner of the room where Bing Crosby, Eddie Fisher, Joey Bishop, Jerry Lester, Harry Rose, Frank Ross, Alan Gale, Eddie Schaffer, Morty Gunty and Eddie Cantor were holding forth.

Old Banjo Eyes hasn't lost his touch. He drew the biggest laugh with this one:

Two psychiatrists were talking shop. Inevitably, the conversation got down to specific cases.

"You think you got problems," said one after listening to his colleague's tale of woe. "I've been conducting a testing program among my patients. You should live so long!"

"What sort of test?" asked his friend.

"Well, I'll try out a few questions on you. What would you say if I asked you what wears a skirt and employs the lips to give pleasure?"

"I'd say a Scotch bagpiper."

"And you'd be right. Next question: what has streamlined curves and arouses the most basic instincts in man?"

"A roller coaster?"

"Of course. Now, what's warm and soft and a pleasure to share a bed with?"

"A hot water bottle, of course."

"What else? But you should hear some of the crazy answers I get from my patients!"

☺

In the far corner of the room there was another all-star huddle. The circumference of this circle was composed of Joe E. Lewis, Ray Bloch, Cy Reeves, Lenny Kenty, Joey Adams, Benny Fields, Jackie Kannon, Ken Kling, Sidney and Harold Gary, Phil Spitalny, Harry Hershfield, Carl Timin, Harry Delf and Danny Thomas. I poked my head in long enough to tell them this one:

The scholarly-looking little man seemed out of place in night court. Charged with being a Peeping Tom, the hapless fellow had been caught red-handed with a pair of binoculars trained on a window across the court.

"You have been charged with spying on the girls at the Emerson Residence Hall. How do you plead?" the magistrate challenged.

"Not guilty, Your Honor."

"Just a minute," interrupted the arresting officer. "We caught this guy with a pair of binoculars focussed right on a window where a girl was undressing. He can't pretend he's innocent!"

"I was simply indulging in my hobby," countered the accused self-righteously.

"Hobby, is it?" sneered the man on the bench. "Well, I suppose counterfeiting could be called a hobby, but it's still against the law."

"My avocation happens to be ornithology," sniffed the defendant. "I am a bird-watcher."

"That's a new one!" roared the judge. "And your binoculars slipped, I suppose, and accidentally got focussed on the bedroom of a semi-nude blonde?"

"Not at all," replied the accused haughtily. "The blonde you mention is a very ordinary example of her species. But, now, you take her parakeet . . . !"

☺

I had no sooner delivered the punch line than Milton Berle, the abbot of the Friars, sneaked up from behind and grabbed me by the arm.

"Surprise, surprise," he giggled, as he led me to the door followed by the gang of suddenly-silenced jokesters.

He gestured toward a brand-new Cadillac parked in front of the house. "Myron, the boys of the Friars decided you should have a beautiful car to match your lovely new home," said he solemnly.

"Gee, fellows," I muttered, all choked up, "I hardly know what to say."

"Don't try, old man, don't try," said Dean of the Friars Harry Delf, patting me gently on the shoulder. He handed me a small book. "This goes with the car," he explained.

"What's it about?" I asked, touched. "I suppose it tells how to take care of the car?"

188

"Sort of," piped up Jack Leonard. "Every time you make a payment, they'll tear a coupon out of it."

And so it went. It was a housewarming that really lived up to its name, what with all the hot ones that scorched the air between midnight and dawn. Yes, the Friars are a great bunch. I was only sorry all the boys couldn't make it that night. Oh, I did have one small complaint: what with all those familiar Friar

faces, plus the effect of the "refreshments" they brought with them, and the old school feeling of the scene, I got a little confused about time and place. Maybe it was my conscience for putting it off, or the sentimentality that oozed from my pores—but whatever it was, I kept insisting on paying my dues. I don't know if it was three or four, five or six, or even twenty times. And I paid in cash . . . so I'll never know. . . .

As I've said before, *seriously,* I liked the job of selling silk, but selling laughs isn't work to me. It's still hard for me to realize that I can make a living on humor after those years of giving it away. Now those customers who wouldn't give me orders after they'd laughed at my jokes have to pay to see me perform. What bliss! Meanwhile, I hope you've enjoyed all this; and if you smiled and chuckled as you read, you'll howl when you see me in person. After all, even my mother did the first time she looked me in the face. It's the only one of its kind.